PSYCHIC ENERGY
How to Change Desires into Realities

JOSEPH J. WEED

PARKER PUBLISHING COMPANY, INC.

West Nyack, N.Y.

A Word from the Author

We are today just beginning to emerge from the repression and superstition that have limited human thought for over a thousand years. The concept of freedom, for example, is cherished by all and many even believe that because they enjoy a certain freedom of action they are truly free. Yet many of the ancient inhibitions are still with us, confining most men's minds more rigidly than prison bars and chains, depriving them of attaining their desires.

Up to fairly recent times, any occurrence not clearly physical in nature was regarded as supernatural. It had to be either the work of the devil and therefore evil, or if not, then that of an angel or saint. A woman gifted with precognition was branded a witch and usually burned to death if she was so unwise as to reveal her ability. Only under the aspect of and in the language of an accepted religion dared a man with etheric vision describe what he saw. The possibility that he might be displaying a normal human ability was beyond belief. And many, regrettably, still cannot accept this.

It is high time we all grew up. We all possess "gifts of the spirit" as St. Paul described them. When we begin to regard these gifts for what they actually are, human abilities that need but to be encouraged, we will find ourselves on the threshold of a new, richer and more exciting life.

In the pages that follow certain more obvious parapsychological "gifts" are described and instructions for your development of them given. There are many others, but to all, *psychic energy* is the key. Train yourself to recognize this energy—to feel it—and learn to build it up within you. It will enable you to perform seeming miracles, which are fully described in this book. But more than this, it will lead you to become a greater and better human being.

That you may strive to and achieve your heart's desires is my earnest wish for you!

Joseph J. Weed

Contents

*How You Can Achieve Psychic Projection
By Employing Psychic Energy*

Involuntary psychic projection. Etheric projection. Mental projection. Techniques to follow to accomplish mental projection. Training case histories. Astral projection. Methods of training for astral projection. The nature of the astral plane and its relation to the physical.

*How to Employ Psychic Energy to Raise
Your Consciousness to Higher Levels*

"Lift up your thoughts" say all religious teachers. What this actually means and how to go about it. The great need to raise the physical vibratory level along with the astral and mental. The practice of any one or more of the techniques described herein will raise the vibrations in your entire atomic structure. The current plan of God for humanity. The thinning of the veil and how you may benefit by it. A final marvelous exercise which if performed daily will enable you to raise your consciousness to a point where you, too, may see through the veil.

1

How Psychic Energy
Manifests Itself

In February 1942 two men sat talking with each other in one of the business clubs in Toronto, Canada. They were discussing Franklin D. Roosevelt, then president of the United States. One, an American, was criticizing Roosevelt. "He is a vain man and often jeopardizes the welfare of his country to satisfy this vanity," he said, "and furthermore he frequently misstates facts and publicly lies about his intentions. He swore to keep us out of war, for example, yet people love him even though he did not. I don't know how he does it."

"You underrate him," his Canadian host replied. "You see his weaknesses because they are familiar to you, they are akin to your own weaknesses. He is the victim of certain human frailties, just as we all are. But of his strength you know nothing because you have but little of it yourself and do not recognize what you do not understand. Roosevelt commands vast amounts of psychic energy and this is what enables him to sway people.

THE POWER TO INFLUENCE OTHERS THROUGH PSYCHIC ENERGY

"I know Roosevelt well," continued the Canadian. "He is a charmer. Everyone who has had to deal with him or negotiate with him has felt this. And he can turn this charm on and off just as easily as you can turn the switch of the motor in your car."

"You believe this?" the American asked.

"I know it," was the reply. "Some years ago he negotiated the threatened strike of the musicians union against the radio networks and stations. Music, then, as it is now, was the life blood of radio broadcasting, so the strike ordered by the union head, James C. Petrillo, was a serious threat. Yet Petrillo was demanding increases and concessions which were at the time impossible for the radio stations to grant. At this point Roosevelt requested that Petrillo and the representatives of the radio networks meet with him at the White House. Because of my interest in Canadian broadcasting, which would inevitably be affected by any contracts made with the musicians in the United States, I went to Washington but was not a part of the conference.

"I talked with Petrillo at his hotel before he went to see Roosevelt. He struck me as a vain little guy but a man of great determination and considerable power. It was my judgment that he would get all he asked. When I saw him immediately after the conference, he was a changed man. He seemed slightly dazed and he repeated more than once: 'He called me Jimmy! Me, little Jimmy Petrillo from Chicago, and the President calls me Jimmy!' Petrillo had given in on every difficult point, yet the settlement was a fair one. The musicians achieved many of their objectives but in such a way that the networks could grant them without being too greatly penalized. It was another Roosevelt triumph! Both parties to the compromise settlement were happy and all came out of the meeting with a warm personal regard for Roosevelt.

"This is but one example of Roosevelt's unusual power," continued the Canadian. "Everyone who knows him can attest to some similar evidence of his ability to win people over to his point of view. Few people, though, know the secret of this charm. They attribute it to personal magnetism or strong personality and think no more about it. Yet Roosevelt consciously and deliberately employed psychic energy to achieve his objectives. This I now know."

"How do you know this?" asked the American.

"Because I have learned to employ this same psychic energy myself," came the surprising reply.

The American's interest increased. His Canadian friend was a man of great wealth and world-wide interests. If he used psychic energy, as he said Roosevelt did, and it helped him achieve the success he obviously enjoyed, this was something worth knowing. So he asked, "Is this psychic energy a quality, an ability given only to a few, like great strength or musical genius, or might a man like myself learn to use it?"

The answer surprised and pleased him. "Psychic energy," said tho Canadian, "is humanity's greatest treasure. It is available to every man and everyone uses it to a greater or lesser degree, usually without realizing it. But just as a champion athlete trains his muscles, his coordination and his endurance, so everyone can increase his store of psychic energy and learn how to use it."

"Could I learn?" asked the American.

"Of course," came the immediate reply, "and if you like I will help you get started."

This was a flattering offer but in the American's mind there was still doubt. How could he, a simple person, an ordinary man, hope to attain to the greatness of a president or to the wealth and power of this man before him? So he said, "Of course, Roosevelt is president and the authority of the office carries a great deal of weight. Surely, this must be what has impressed Petrillo and others."

"No one can dispute the glamour and power of presidential authority," answered his companion. "But Roosevelt has and uses more than this. Let me tell you a story about another man, a man like yourself, in fact a man you know, Ian K." And he proceeded to tell this strange story about a man the American knew quite well.

HOW PSYCHIC ENERGY WAS USED TO BUILD A FORTUNE

Ian had come to work for the wealthy Canadian about six years previously. He started as a salesman on commission and soon proved himself. It was about this time his employer discovered the principles behind the functioning of psychic energy and began to use them in furthering his own career. He had three or four small businesses in northern Ontario, all very much alike. So as an experiment he introduced Ian to the basic principles underlying the use of psychic energy and encouraged him to study them. At the same time he put him in charge of one of these small businesses and gave him a twenty percent interest in it.

Within three years, Ian had so built up this business that it was worth about five times its original value, while the other similar ventures in the same area had increased in value only thirty to forty percent.

The owner regarded this as unquestionable evidence of the power of psychic energy and he was quite pleased with his little experiment. But he was in for a surprise. Ian came to him and told him he was leaving because he wanted to go into business for himself. "And I want you to buy back from me the twenty percent interest in the business which you gave me," he said.

At this point in his story the Canadian said, "The remarkable thing was that I didn't resent it at all. I could see the reasonableness of his position so I offered him $100,000 for his 20% and he took it. I knew in my heart what was going on but I couldn't help feeling that I wanted to help him become a great success and this was the first major step."

Armed with the $100,000 Ian came to Toronto and contracted to buy a very large business. The price was many times the money he had, but he called upon several Toronto businessmen, all previously unknown to him, and persuaded each to lend him a portion of the money required to complete the transaction. This in itself is an amazing evidence of the power of psychic energy. A young man who three years before did not have two nickels to rub together comes into Toronto and seeks out several of the wealthiest and most successful men in the city. They not only meet and talk with him but they actually lend him money, over half a million dollars! True, the business he was buying was offered as security, but anyone who has tried to borrow money on this basis can tell you how difficult it is and what a large part confidence in the ability of the individual plays.

"You know Ian," concluded the Canadian, "and you have done business with him. You know he has recently bought two more large businesses and is today regarded as one of the richest and most successful young men in all Canada."

The American did indeed know him and when he heard this story his doubts dissolved. He asked the older man to tell him about psychic energy, how he might accumulate it and how he might learn to use it. Kindly, generously, his host began to tell him what he wanted to know. They talked that night, and the next and the next, until finally the younger man felt equipped to pursue the study on his own.

All of this is completely true. It actually took place and I remember it quite well because, as you suspect, the young American was myself. In relating it here, I have not mentioned the identity of the older man and I have changed the name of his young protege because these men are alive today and are indeed quite prominent.

BENEFITS SECURED WITH PSYCHIC ENERGY

In the course of those three lengthy conversations I learned a great deal. My tutor pointed out that the ability to win others to your point of view, without their realizing they are being influenced, is only one of the powerful manifestations of psychic energy. There are countless others. Most of the strange and seemingly inexplicable abilities that are today coming more and more to public notice are the result of the application of psychic energy in one way or another. Mental telepathy, dowsing, finding lost articles or missing persons, levitation, psychic projection, all are evidences of the power of psychic energy. All of these so-called "unknown talents" and more will be explained in detail in later chapters and you will be instructed in the techniques required to perform these seemingly miraculous acts.

USE OF PSYCHIC ENERGY AVAILABLE FOR ANYONE

Let me state here that nothing to be described in this book is supernormal, beyond the abilities of the average human being. These are not miracles, if a miracle is defined as "a mysterious event in the natural world but out of its established order, possible only by the intervention of a divine power," to quote Funk and

Wagnall's dictionary. But they are surely "strange and wondrous things" to the average man unaware of the means employed to perform them.

At one point in the conversations with my tutor (as I came to regard him) I asked, "Why have you taken the time and the trouble to explain these things to me? You owe me nothing."

He replied, "Knowledge of psychic energy brings with it certain responsibilities, one of which is to impart this knowledge to others. This was not always so. At one time in the world's history it was necessary for this knowledge to be kept secret and shared only with a trusted few. But today that dark hour has passed and there are thousands alive who are competent to assume this responsibility. Their number is increasing daily as the minds of men become more open and their hearts more tolerant and compassionate. Thus I have shared what I know with Ian and with others and I eagerly give it to you. I know you well enough to realize you will employ it with restraint and dignity and the time will come when it will be possible for you to pass it on to many, many others."

I now know what he meant by that last sentence but I did not comprehend it at the time. Today, twenty-five years later, the world is a different place and the consciousness of humanity has expanded. All over the world there are men and women with open minds eagerly awaiting this knowledge, responsible people who will employ it to raise themselves and their environment to higher levels of living and thinking. You, the reader, are such a person. The fact that you have selected this book and are reading these words is evidence that you have within you a spark that needs but little fanning to bring it to flame. This small magnet has drawn you to this book and the book to you. There are thousands, hundreds of thousands like you all over the world. For you and for them this book has been written so that the knowledge, kept so long for only the select few, may be spread far and wide, that humanity may realize, at last, its innate abilities and open the door to the Golden Age.

THE NATURE OF ENERGY

There are three basic energies. Very few persons are aware of more than one type. Science recognizes *physical energy* only, and everything that can be seen, felt or measured, falls into this category. Further, this includes not only human muscular energy but solar energy, gravity, magnetism, atomic energy, electricity, steam, and so on. All these are manifestations of physical energy.

Of a much finer grade than physical energy, and as different from physical energy as air is different from rock, is *psychic energy.* Being of a higher vibratory essence than any physical energy, psychic energy can dominate and use physical energy. *Psychic energy is man's particular gift.* On this planet, only man may *consciously* use it. It is humanity's greatest treasure.

You have this priceless gift and you have used it, maybe deliberately and with full awareness, but much more likely without any realization of the technique employed. Very few people consciously wield psychic energy, but it is my purpose in this book to teach you how to take hold of it and use it for your benefit. When you are able to do this, your consciousness will expand and *you will become aware of things you presently only dimly comprehend or do not recognize at all.* You will be able to sway and influence people, you will be able to project your thoughts into the minds of others in such a way that they will regard them as their own ideas, you will be able to dominate physical energy and lead it to accomplish seeming miracles, and you will be able to do countless other strange and wonderful things. Instructions for all this and more you will find in the chapters that follow.

The third basic energy is what is known as Primal Energy. It is as far beyond psychic energy as psychic energy is beyond physical energy. Primal Energy might be described as the building blocks of the entire manifested universe. It is not the light and heat of the sun, but the energy from which this light and heat are derived. It is the cohesive energy in the tiny atom which, when forced apart, translates itself into the powerful physical manifestation of an atomic explosion. It is everywhere. It interpenetrates and gives both substance and action to all. From the human point of view it is infinite. It assumes all forms—physical, emotional, mental, spiritual. It provides all movement from the growing of a leaf to the explosion of a star. If we assume an infinite First Cause, the Primal Energy is the plastic molded by Its Will, the Binah of the Kabbalist, the Mother of the World of the Buddhist, the Holy Ghost of the Christians. But of this Primal Energy we will have little to say because our concern here is to work with the more immediate possibilities of psychic energy.

HOW TO BEGIN TO PUT PSYCHIC ENERGY INTO ACTION

As children we used to amuse ourselves in school and in other gatherings by gazing fixedly at the back of the head of someone in front of us in order to make that person turn around. It almost always worked. Even when the head didn't actually turn there was usually a fidgeting or some other sign of uneasiness. You have surely done the same at one time or another. The energy you used to impress the other person was psychic energy.

You have often heard the expression, "Energy follows thought." This usually means psychic energy, and in the foregoing small experiment the eye under the direction of the mind is used to concentrate psychic energy on the head or neck of the person in front. If you have never done this, try it the next time you are in a group where the minds of people are temporarily at rest. Of course, in the theatre during an exciting stage performance or when a motion picture is on the screen, the attention of the audience is held transfixed, but in any lull between acts or pictures it will work. You can thus prove to yourself the existence of psychic energy and your own ability to use it. This will give you confidence and make more easy the attainment of the benefits which will be described in later chapters.

Now let me tell you exactly how to do this. First, the person must be in front of you or, if at one side, at least far enough forward so you can see the back of his or her head. Second, the person must be at ease and relaxed. You can do this in a theatre for example between the acts or before the performance. It can be done in a schoolroom, in a library, or an office, in fact in any place where the subject is not engaged in something exciting or so interesting that it will absorb his or her entire attention. All you need do then is fix your gaze upon the lower part of the back of the subject's head at about the point where it joins the neck. Just look and silently wish to yourself, "I wish he (or she) would turn around." Keep looking steadily and within a minute or two, if your own attention has not been disturbed, your subject will start to fidget a bit and usually will turn right around and look in your direction.

Don't think of "energy" or of "sending any force." Just look and wish. Try this several times in different circumstances and on different people. You will notice a variety of results. This is because people are not alike and also because you yourself are different from time to time and function with varying degrees of efficiency. If you persist with this experiment, and it should be nothing more than that, you will notice that your own skill increases. You will get better and quicker results which will not be difficult to relate to the improvement in the technique you employ. You will also find that you gradually become aware that you are consciously using some sort of force.

Try the foregoing experiment several times. With each success your confidence will increase and prepare you to perform more complicated tasks. For, if you follow the programs in this book you can train yourself to do many things that the average scientist will tell you are impossible and which the average person will look upon as miracles.

HOW TO INFLUENCE OTHERS TO HELP YOU

You can exert personality influence, as has been suggested. However, this does not mean that you can compel someone to do your bidding against his will. Not at all. But it does mean that if you have a worthy objective, you can get people necessary to the success of your plans to fall in with your ideas and, in fact, to actually want to help you. This is the best way. The voluntary cooperation of others makes the pathway to success much, much smoother. The ability to influence others may be developed in many ways. Two of the best methods will be described in detail in a later chapter.

THE PROTECTION AND PHYSICAL BENEFITS OF PSYCHIC ENERGY

A not-too-often recognized virtue of psychic energy is its use as a personal protective force. Properly organized and employed with clear intent, psychic energy can protect you from physical harm, from emotional storms and mental attacks. Advanced workers tell that they use it to guard themselves against excessive heat or great cold. Of course it is foolish to carry this unusual ability to the point of fanaticism, as do certain Tibetan monks who step

nude into below zero cold and endeavor to melt the snow around
them by the power of their energies. Nearer to home and on a
lesser scale we have the "snow birds," the men and women who
take an ocean bath each day throughout the winter. These people
believe that the bath keeps them healthy—but it is actually their
willful accumulation of psychic energy to keep themselves warm
that results in improved vigor and physical well-being.

The more psychic energy you demand, the more you get. When
supply exceeds normal needs for a month or two, certain physical
changes begin to take place. You gain much more control over
your physical equipment. Your eyesight and hearing improve
along with your physical coordination, but in addition you will
notice that you feel lighter. You will be able to run upstairs rapidly,
sometimes two steps at a time with no great effort, and advanced
practitioners can often levitate, that is raise themselves completely
off the ground. Because of its interest to many people I have included a chapter on levitation and the techniques required to
accomplish it.

DEVELOPING TELEPATHIC ABILITY AND PSYCHIC SENSITIVITY

As you begin to accumulate psychic energy and put it to use,
you will observe that you are becoming increasingly sensitive to
the emotions and thoughts of others. At first it will seem that you
are aware only that a person is pleased or displeased with something you have said or done and you will attribute it to observation of a facial expression or a physical attitude. But as this becomes clearer and you are conscious of more subtle responses,
you will be forced to recognize that you are actually "picking up"
an emotional emanation or a thought radiating from the other.
This is the beginning of telepathic rapport. Everyone is capable
of it and many are quite competent without fully realizing just
what they are doing or how they are doing it. It is possible to
send thoughts to others as well as receive them and this whole
technique is fully described in the chapter devoted to telepathy.

Akin to telepathy but on a different level is the ability to tune
in on people, places, animals and things. Today we read often of
remarkable individuals like the Dutchman Croiset, Washington's

Jeane Dixon or the amazing Edgar Cayce. All used psychic energy to reach out and make contact with the desired objective. Thus Croiset found lost people and valuable objects, Jeane Dixon found a new home, and Edgar Cayce could describe with accuracy the illness of a man a thousand miles away.

A simple application of this same faculty is the ability to dowse for underground water and other riches. Seven out of ten people can do this with little or no training. Psychic energy is used and needed but not more than the average person can supply. A whole chapter is devoted to the development of this ability to the point where it becomes a skill and may be used as a trade or business. This technique will work not only to find water but also oil, minerals, caves and almost anything for which the location is unknown. The marines in Vietnam have been using an adaptation of the dowsing technique to locate enemy tunnels and booby traps. When their seismic detectors were knocked out of commission by heavy bombardment, the men took over with dowsing rods improvised from metal coat hangers and successfully prevented underground infiltration by the Viet Cong.

HOW TO TELL TIME WITHOUT A TIMEPIECE

Here is a simple experiment you can perform without apparatus right in your own home. Once you have learned how to do this and have developed a little skill, you will always be able to do it. You will never forget it. It is nothing more or less than telling time without looking at a clock or watch. In brief, you use psychic energy to reach out and contact a specific clock and bring back to your mind the time that clock is recording at that moment. It's really very simple. Here's how to do it:

Let us say you wake up in the night and wish to know the time. With your eyes closed, visualize the clock at which you would normally look, not the clock in the kitchen but the one closest to your bed. See its face in your mind's eye and observe where the hands point. Then open your eyes, turn on the light and look. See how close you have come. Now let me warn you about something. When you start to visualize the clock face, you will almost certainly start to "guess" the time. Don't do this! It is fatal to the success of what you are attempting because it brings the brain in as an interfering agent. This ability to tell time exactly has nothing to do with reasoning power. The more you try to "reason" to the exact time, the worse you will get. What you are to do is to actually *look*, not reason, not guess, but look at the clock. Visualize the clock face by sending a ray of psychic energy to it which will return to your mind's eye a completely accurate reproduction of the appearance of the clock face at that moment.

With a little practice you will catch on. It's a little like learning to swim or riding a bicycle. You make several tries and then suddenly you know. Once you know, you will never forget. When you have confidence, you need never look at a clock except to reconfirm what you already know.

PSYCHOMETRY AS POWERED WITH PSYCHIC ENERGY

Somewhat akin to the finding of lost articles and the discovery of underground minerals and waters is the ability to psychometrize. This is a method of gaining information about a person by holding in your hand an object that has been worn or carried by that person. As has been explained, everyone has a store of psychic energy, some more, some less. This energy radiates in a physical, magnetic manner and has a tendency to adhere to material objects. A gold watch or a silver bracelet will collect and retain a measurable amount of the energy radiated by its owner and when you have been sensitized you will be able to discern it. From this contact you can learn a great deal about the wearer, his or her character. Certain thoughts and ideas, and not infrequently pictures of events in that person's past, will present themselves to your mind's eye.

This technique is sometimes called psychometry and can be acquired through practice once you have an understanding of psychic energy and an adequate supply. A later chapter is devoted to this subject and contains not only instructions but some interesting examples of how psychometry works.

PSYCHIC PROJECTION

Today one reads a great deal about astral projection or psychic projection. This is the ability to send the mind or the consciousness to a distant point while the physical body lies quietly at home in a sleeping or trance-like condition. While away on these "missions" the mind or consciousness becomes aware of, and can record and bring back, a memory of what is observed. From some of the things being written or said about this amazing feat one might be led to believe it is a relatively simple accomplishment. Let me tell you, it is not that simple.

It can be done and many people have learned how, but this requires study, practice and a great ability to concentrate. But it is important that you know and understand this, so there are two chapters devoted to its explanation and study, one on what is usually referred to as mental projection and the other on astral projection. They are vastly different, and indeed each technique embraces many subtleties and varying shades of action. Entire books can be written about astral projection alone and it is obvious therefore that full justice cannot be done to the subject in one or two chapters. But it is my purpose to condense enough information into this book to enable you to understand projection and even to start some experiments with it. Then, if this is a subject which interests you and to which you are willing to devote the necessary time and effort, more complete instruction will be made available.

HOW PSYCHIC DEVELOPMENT LEADS TO PRECOGNITION

Through training you will increase your store of psychic energy and the ability to wield it. Soon you will come to recognize in advance that certain things are about to happen. At first these will be simple and seemingly so inconsequential that you are apt to overlook them. In driving your car to the movies or the supermarket you will suddenly be certain that you will find a parking place in the most desirable spot and it will happen that, as you drive up, a car will move out and leave a convenient space. Or it may be that as you arise in the morning you will think of someone you have not seen for several months and the conviction will reach you that you will hear from that person during the day. And this will occur.

From these seemingly simple and unimportant "precognitions" you will proceed to much larger and more significant observations. No particular training or practice is needed to develop this. All that is necessary is to have confidence. Do not reject the premonitions, but keep an open mind and the training in psychic energy to which you are applying yourself will then bring with it an added benefit—this prophetic tendency. There are many other so-called fringe benefits that will be yours as you apply yourself to this work. Good health, freedom from disease, and increased endurance will become so normal to you as to pass almost without comment. So I urge you, in your own interest, to study carefully the instructions given and to devote some time and effort to acquiring the skills described. This small amount of bread cast upon the waters will be returned to you a thousandfold.

2

Techniques To Increase and Control Your Psychic Energy

Psychic energy is not a commodity like a breakfast food that you can buy off a shelf in a supermarket. It is not something you gain as the result of sounding a magic word. You already possess psychic energy! Yes, and you use it, albeit unknowingly—maybe not often or to any great degree. But you have it and use it because you are a human being and *every human being possesses the treasure of psychic energy*

What is important to you now is that I can tell you how to increase your normal store of psychic energy. This is somewhat in the nature of increasing your capacity and then employing special techniques to fill that enlarged capacity. I can also show you how to prevent wasteful losses of psychic energy. Best of all, I can teach you how to lay hold of and manipulate psychic energy in order that you may obtain the things you want from life. But I can't give you this energy. If I could, I would. But you are so constituted that *the only way you can get it is through your own efforts*.

We all possess a very human weakness. We would all like to

get something for nothing, or at least get a lot from a little effort. But in this world you get just about what you pay for. The amazing and most rewarding quality of psychic energy is that a small additional supply, properly directed, will bring manifest results out of all proportion to the initial effort. But you must make the effort. Let me tell you another true story about a man who made this effort and the great benefits it brought him.

HOW A SALES MANAGER REACHED THE TOP OF HIS COMPANY

At the time he and I first discussed psychic energy and he decided to apply it, he was working as the sales manager of one of the divisions of a very large corporation. This company is so large its sales from all ten divisions run to nearly a billion dollars annually. My friend was competent, well-trained and hard-working, *but in this respect no different from nearly one hundred other young executives in the company.*

My own success with psychic energy, and the reports I was able to give him of the benefits others had achieved, inspired him to make a vigorous effort to employ it in his own behalf. The results were amazing and almost immediate. In a few short years he rose to be general sales manager of all divisions; then he was made vice-president in charge of sales. Two years later, upon the retirement of the president, he was elected to that office and within another eighteen months was chosen by the directors for the highest office in this multi-million-dollar company, that of chairman of the board.

Not too long ago, he and his wife joined my wife and me for dinner and over coffee, as the two women chatted about their children, he suddenly became serious.

"Joe," he said, "some decisions take more out of a man than a month's hard labor. I'm facing a tough one and it has me exhausted."

I had known throughout the meal that he had something on his mind but this was not unusual. Each day he had to solve problems and make decisions that affected not only the welfare of the business and the income of the stockholders but also the individual interest of every employee. So I waited in silence, knowing there was more to come.

"It's about this mine purchase," he said. "The details are not clear. Oh, I have plenty of facts and under one set of developing conditions, it's a wise move. But there is no certainty or even sound probability that things will go that way. In fact it seems about an even chance either way."

I knew what he referred to. His company converted raw materials into finished and semi-finished products. Some sources of this raw material were mines which they owned, but these only supplied a fraction of their total output. Through his own unique ability he had negotiated the purchase of a huge mine which occupied an entire mountain and was the largest single source of the material his company used. Now he was faced with the need to decide whether or not to recommend to his directors that the purchase be consummated. The crux of the problem lay in the fact that it required, among other things, the outlay of $45,000,000.

I said to him, "How do you feel about it yourself?"

"I think we should buy it," he answered quickly. "I have felt all along that it will be a great forward step for our company but there are some who think otherwise."

I knew he meant his bankers. But they are always conservative by nature, so I said, "If you feel it is right, how can you doubt its wisdom? Surely your own recent experiences must give you confidence in your judgment."

He understood my reference. It was psychic energy which had guided him to the right decision in many major issues and the keen judgment he displayed had indeed been the reason for his rapid advancement. Even now he hardly needed the encouragement I gave him. He bought the mine and, in the face of subsequent rising prices, this move was hailed as his greatest and most brilliant achievement.

The reason I relate this story is to give you an example of how psychic energy sharpens the judgment. And it also gives you the confidence and courage to go ahead with plans you conceive to be right.

Psychic energy is another term for "soul energy." This is not a religious concept but very practical human equipment. Every one has and uses psychic energy to a greater or lesser degree. The person with a dynamic personality, a personality infused with enthusiasm, wields a great deal of this amazing energy. You can acquire such a personality and the enthusiasm that sweeps all before it by developing your ability to manipulate it. Let me tell you how to do this.

HOW TO DEVELOP YOUR PSYCHIC ENERGY

The first and most important step in the development of psychic energy is to recognize that it exists. Most educated people are aware that there is something called psychic energy, or soul energy, but they do not think of it in relation to themselves. They do not see it as a power inherent in them that can be employed consciously to improve their health and make them more successful. Before you can hope to benefit to any degree from psychic energy you must first know what it is and what it can do. Then the second step is to think about it, to be aware of it and turn your mind to it as naturally as you would extend your hand to pick up a glass of water. This, of course, requires many conscious repetitions before it becomes habitual.

Man has known about psychic energy for a long, long time. All the great religions refer to it. Some call it the Grace of God, others Soul Force, and still others refer to it as Cosmic Energy. The Great Teachers and Avatars used different images to convey this idea, images which varied according to their own imaginations and also according to the level of understanding of the people whom they taught. The scientific developments of the present century, particularly those in electronics, have so informed our minds that today a much clearer and more accurate understanding of psychic energy is possible. While it is quite true that this energy can be, and often is, bestowed as a gift by a higher being, it is also possible for each person to generate his own supply and learn to control it.

If you believe that soul energy is something strange, remote and relatively unattainable, dispel this notion immediately. This is yesterday's concept and as out of date as yesterday's newspaper. It is a relic of the old Piscean idea that everyone had to be helped in order to develop. Cast it aside. Today, everyone can help himself—you can help yourself to a greater, fuller life, to more energy and to success in all your most cherished projects.

For some things, you use psychic energy as simply and naturally as physical energy without realizing it. Do you own a dog? Have you ever ridden a horse? When you command a dog to lie down, to be quiet, to guard, you are transmitting not only a vocal message but also a psychic command. When little Kathy Kusner, our Olympic champion horsewoman, who weighs only about 100 pounds, takes command of a horse, 1500 pounds of powerful bone and muscle, she is the boss. It is the psychic energy she employs which enables her to so control the animal beneath her that it responds immediately and sensitively to her slightest wish. What I am trying to convey to you is that psychic energy is yours to command. Once you understand and accept this idea, you are well on your way.

HOW TO ADD TO YOUR STORE OF PSYCHIC ENERGY

It is possible to increase your normal intake of psychic energy in three ways, through food or other nourishment, through the air you breathe, and by use of the mind, heart and other centers. Let us first talk about nourishment.

There are three physical organs which transform into psychic energy the food energy taken into the system. These are the spleen, the appendix and the heart. The appendix, which modern medicine holds valueless and removes on the slightest excuse, is actually a transformer of energy. You can get along without it and many do. But with it functioning properly, you can add much more quickly to your psychic energy store.

The spleen and heart will function after surgery and continue to perform physical service, but their value as psychic transformers will be seriously impaired, if not destroyed, by the knife. The efficiency of all three may be greatly enhanced by proper thought. If you view them mentally as transformers and suggest to yourself that they are using physical energy to attract psychic energy while food is being digested, their action will be multiplied many times.

The partaking of food was regarded as a sacred ceremony by the ancients. They considered it so important that a proper atmosphere had to prevail whenever food was consumed. You know from your own experience how indigestion has followed a meal eaten when you were nervous, upset, frightened or angry. Any food partaken in an emotionally charged atmosphere results not only in physical distress but also in a great waste of psychic energy. The physical evidence, serious though it may be, is only a dim reflection of the psychic disturbance. Not without reason do many households proclaim, "Never bring your troubles to the table." These people are wise. They know that a meal eaten in tranquility, in a warm and jovial atmosphere, is more easily digested—but more than this, though not often realized, the psychic energy of each participant is increased.

This sounds almost too simple. You ask, "Do you mean to tell me I can increase my store of psychic energy just by remaining calm during meals?" The answer is, "Yes, you can." But on reflection and after trying a few times, you will realize this is not so simple. It is not easy to change the habits of a lifetime. Nor can you always prevent others from burdening you with their troubles and emotional problems at meal time.

Do you read the paper at breakfast? Stop it. Do you occasionally read a book or a business document while lunching or even just munching a sandwich? If you do, stop it. Do not delude yourself that you are saving time in this way. You are not. From a purely physical point of view, the division of attention robs both your stomach and brain of needed blood. Not only is your digestion impaired but your entire mental action is dulled and slowed down. Furthermore, instead of an increase in your psychic energy which a nourishing meal should bring, your inner being has to draw upon its reserves to help support the simultaneously increased activity of stomach, eyes and brain.

It will become more and more clear to you as you continue this study that your thoughts and your mental attitude have a great deal to do with your supply of psychic energy. When eating, bear in mind that the good food you are taking into your system has the capacity to attract psychic energy in addition to supplying you with physical sustenance. A conscious realization of this will result in a greater supply than if you give it no thought at all. This contrasts sharply with the loss of psychic energy which is suffered when food is eaten under tension or other adverse conditions. The discovery of vitamins and their great value as a dietary supplement was a remarkable nutritional breakthrough. Yet the efficiency of vitamins may actually be enhanced if they are consumed with a conscious realization of the benefit they bring. Taken in tranquility and with proper thought they become the basic ingredients of physical wellbeing and increased psychic energy. But the converse is also true. Just as good food, consumed in fear or anger, becomes poisonous, so vitamins taken when irritated or upset will fail to benefit and may actually increase irritability.

It is obvious that food contains energy—and to a more concentrated degree so do vitamins. But this is purely unconscious energy which comes into your system ready to perform whatever task you assign it. It strengthens and accumulates at any point and in any way that consciousness may direct. Realization multiplies all energies. Sunlight provides heat, but in order to cause a paper to break into flame, a focusing lens is needed. In the same way, while psychic energy radiates naturally from every organism that possesses it, in order to benefit you must learn to gather and focus it consciously. Your mind must become the focusing lens. Thus it is necessary to discriminate between the unconscious flow of psychic energy and the sharpened arrow of precisely directed consciousness.

These are the ABC's of the study of psychic energy. They must be understood and accepted before you can learn to apply the more sophisticated techniques which will be given later in this chapter. But there are other simple sources of psychic energy which are available to everyone. Let me tell you of one or two before going on to more advanced considerations.

OTHER SOURCES OF PSYCHIC ENERGY

Conifer-bearing evergreens of the pine and cedar families radiate pure psychic energy. This fact is but dimly realized. True, certain doctors recommend that patients with weak lungs change their home to the vicinity of a pine forest, while others suggest sleeping on pillows filled with balsam needles. There are also concoctions made from pine sap which are designed to alleviate coughs and throat irritations. But it is extremely doubtful that any real understanding of the values involved exists among the medical profession. Experience has taught that pure air laden with the scent of pines has a strengthening and healing effect on the lungs and that remedies made from turpentine derivations cure throat ailments. Actually it is possible to obtain this energy directly from the living tree, but of course the magnifying lens of your consciousness is needed.

HOW TO OBTAIN PSYCHIC ENERGY FROM TREES

The technique is simple, but your own conscious awareness plays a significant part. Merely touch with your fingertips the sharp ends of the needles on a living pine or cedar branch. Lightly press the balls of the first two fingers and thumb of either hand against the tips of the needles. Retain this hold for two or three minutes while you realize that the energy of the great tree is flowing into you. If you are sensitive you will actually feel this the first time you try it. Certainly if you do it every day for a week you will become aware of increased vitality, more energy and greater endurance. Once you have realized the benefits of this practice you will be encouraged to continue it, and you should. It can only benefit you and you will become healthier and stronger because of it.

I have used the word "healthier" here deliberately. Many of the common human ailments result from a lack of psychic energy. When your nervous energy is at low ebb, gaps appear in your protective "net" of good health. Through these openings all sorts of "intruders" may penetrate and cause various diseases. Thus certain sicknesses can be successfully treated by psychic energy. This is such an important study that a complete chapter is devoted to it later on.

PSYCHIC ENERGY FROM OTHER SUBSTANCES

It is also possible to obtain a supply of psychic energy from small quantities of certain substances. Musk, for example, taken only two to three grains at a time will help restore a depleted stock of psychic energy. This is particularly useful in certain illnesses. I refer here to U. S. P. musk, preferably Tonquin musk. It is quite expensive, in most places about $100 an ounce. However, when it is only used in emergencies and consumed but two or three grains at a time, an ounce lasts quite a while. Only natural U. S. P. musk should ever be taken internally and then in very small amounts. Musk is a secretion of the musk deer or musk ox. Because of its ability to sustain the odor of vegetable essences, it is in great demand in the manufacture of perfumes. This has led to the creation of an artificial musk, a symtrinitro-butyl-toluene compound which has no psychic energy value and must never under any circumstances be taken internally.

Natural musk has been known and used for centuries in India and China. The royalty, rajahs and emperors, would frequently take two or three grains before attending a conference or making an important decision. From experience they knew this helped their minds become clearer and their judgment sounder. It is possible to obtain today the same type of musk used by these potentates a thousand or more years ago. In those days it was a precious substance available only to the rulers and heads of state— today, while expensive, it is available to all.

Valerian is another valuable substance not generally recognized at its true worth. Tincture of valerian is not recommended, but a weak valerian tea which can be brewed at home is very useful. A half cup a day of this weak tea will do much to eliminate poisons from the system and stimulate the glands and other organs which act as transformers of psychic energy. Valerian benefits greatly if taken daily for a week, then skip a week and repeat until two months have elapsed. It should then be discontinued and resumed again in the same manner after six months.

There are many other substances which supply psychic energy in small amounts. Like musk and valerian, they are helpful if you are run down, ill or depleted, and they should be kept in mind for emergencies. But for a person like yourself who wishes to acquire the power of a large supply of psychic energy, a more vigorous approach is needed. This will be discussed after we clear up one more point—how to avoid depleting your store of psychic energy.

HOW TO PREVENT DEPLETION OF PSYCHIC ENERGY

It is only in relatively recent times that the scientific world has begun to understand sleep. For all too long, the only attitude science held toward sleep was that it is nature's way of restoring strength after an exhausting day. You get tired. So you lie down, go to sleep and awake refreshed. No further thought was given it. But in the last few years many able psychologists, psychiatrists and physiologists have become interested in sleep and its concomitant phenomenon, dreaming. Willing human guinea pigs have permitted themselves to be watched throughout all of their sleeping hours and strange changes have been observed. In addition to periodic body shiftings, a phenomenon described as rapid eyeball motion has attracted attention. It is referred to briefly as REM and has been identified with dream activity.

The curious scientists have awakened the sleepers whenever the REM was observed, thus cutting short the dream. They have discovered that if a subject is prevented from dreaming but allowed an otherwise normal eight hours of sleep, he does not get the expected benefit from that sleep. In fact, if dreaming is prevented for several successive nights, the subject becomes irritable and lacking in physical coordination. Some even tend to fall into dreamlike states while at work or at meals, and apparently this is an attempt on the part of the organism to make up the deficiency.

Science is thus, in its usual way, groping from effect to cause. In time it will be known and scientifically accepted that the chief function of sleep is to restore psychic energy. After a day of normal muscular effort and physical energy expenditure, a few hours of rest, without sleep, will restore the physical equipment. But we need more than mere rest. We need sleep because during sleep our psychic energy transformers function with greatest efficiency. As long as our conscious mind is active, as long as we are awake, we are either helping along the accumulation of essential psychic energy or we are wasting it. Since but few people understand how to stimulate the increase of psychic energy, most of us during our waking hours are busy burning it up and destroying it. How? Let me tell you. . . .

All human contact is abrasive. It should not be and you may, at first thought, not agree that it is. But it definitely is and we only ameliorate this roughness by love, affection, compassion and tolerance. As you well know, we don't entertain these noble emotions with all people nor do we experience them at all times, so there are hours and hours every day devoted by us to attack and defense. This has become so habitual that even with no one present, we usually busy ourselves with mental criticisms of actions of others on the international, national, local and personal scene, or concoct future projects designed to enhance our egos or in some other way advance us over our fellow man. These thoughts, words and actions are invariably accompanied by all kinds of emotions. Fear, envy, dislike, resentment, jealousy and irritation are the commonest. They usually get support from pride, vanity and desire. Emotions of this type burn up psychic energy far faster than any human equipment can replace it. Thus if we do not sleep—and dream—we soon run down in all departments. We get nervous, irritable and eventually become prey to disease.

Dreaming is an indication of inner activity and usually, during sleep, this inner activity is the functioning of the heart, spleen and appendix in their work of transforming nourishment into psychic energy. This does not start the moment your head hits the pillow, nor even when you first fall asleep. It is necessary for all of the emotional kinks you have created during the day to straighten themselves out. Then when some semblance of inner relaxation takes place, the transformers begin their necessary pulsation. Most of us dream the greater part of the time we are asleep. This is good. Only a small percentage of these dreams are remembered after waking and some people who never remember claim they do not dream. But their rapid eyeball movements, observed scientifically, indicate some inner mental activity, most likely dreams. So get enough sleep, for it is during sleep that psychic energy is replenished in its fullest quantities.

AGING DUE TO PSYCHIC ENERGY DEPLETION

Young people are usually happier than their elders. They have fewer troubles and worries. Their lives are more serene, so during their working hours they use up less of their precious store of psychic energy. Also they usually sleep longer and thus spend more time restoring what has been lost.

As they grow older and their emotional natures grow up along with their bodies, they are prone to succumb to the various emotional infections to which they are exposed. Most children are infected early by their parents and other elders and pick up from them all sorts of resentments, fears, worries and envies. As these are permitted to gain more and more control of the young adult's thinking, he uses up more psychic energy each day and requires a longer period to replace it each night. But nights are just so long and the tendency, as one grows older, is to get less sleep rather than more. Each day the now-grown man or woman has a fraction less of psychic energy than the day before, and physical aging sets in. The rate of replacement of worn cells in your physical equipment depends upon the amount of psychic energy present. When you destroy cells with low-grade emotions, a great deal of psychic energy is required to stimulate the necessary replacement —the less energy available, the slower the replacement.

This can be documented in many ways. For example, in countries where emotions run high, people age quickly. Women at thirty-five are often old women. Men in those areas last longer chiefly because the need to earn a living requires of them a certain amount of emotional control. On the other hand, in countries where the climate is more rigorous and self-discipline is essential to survival, people grow old gracefully and more slowly. Their physical equipment lasts longer because they give way less often to destructive emotions and retain more psychic energy.

Let me repeat, therefore, that the first major step you must take to increase your store of psychic energy is to stop wasting it. You must make a definite effort to avoid indulging in the so-called negative emotions. Of course this is difficult but a start should be made and the effort renewed periodically.

The best technique is to take a firm grip on yourself, to hold yourself on a tight rein as you would an unruly horse. I know you won't be able to do this continuously and certainly not when your emotions flare high. So I suggest a second method which the ancient Romans called "tactica adversa." It consists in deliberately cultivating a thought directly opposite to the negative emotion. When you feel inclined to be critical, find something to praise. When you are annoyed, look for something to joke or laugh about, even yourself. If you are frightened, tell yourself that tomorrow you will scoff at your fears. When someone hurts you, try to feel compassion for them, not resentment or anger. This is not goody-

goody religiosity but sound psychological advice. If you can act this way, if you even try to act this way, it will help you more than anything else. For in this manner you can cut down your daily wasting of precious psychic energy and gradually increase your supply.

TECHNIQUE FOR INCREASING PSYCHIC ENERGY

Up to this point we have examined the nature of psychic energy, how we normally acquire it and how it is usually dissipated. We have seen that the foods we eat and the air we breathe tend to replenish our psychic energy and that this process is more efficient when we are asleep. We have also seen there are certain substances and living organisms which give off psychic energy or speed up our process of transforming physical into psychic energy.

The destructive life processes have been considered and the debilitating effect of violent emotions explained. All the foregoing are the normal processes which supply or deplete your psychic energy. So now let me give you some suggestions and techniques which will enable you to acquire and store up more-than-normal amounts of this energy. And when you have learned this I will tell you how to put the excess energy to use to accomplish seeming miracles. The two best techniques are:

By means of mind directed breathing.
By mind alone.

Because it is easier to demonstrate, we will study first the technique which employs breath controlled by the mind.

INCREASING PSYCHIC ENERGY BY MEANS OF MIND-CONTROLLED BREATH

Breathing is an automatic function. When the body is at rest, breathing is normally slow and regular. But when violent exercise requires additional oxygen to cleanse the blood stream, the rate and depth of breathing increase automatically. But we can consciously control our rate of breathing, we can slow it down or speed it up at will. We can even stop breathing entirely for short periods. Diving, under-water swimming and water polo require great breath control. The members of the American Olympic Water Polo Team were trained to hold their breath so they could stay under water longer. One barrel-chested athlete had practiced until he was able to hold his breath for more than three minutes and was a great asset to the team—in his case this abnormal breath retention enabled him to lurk on the bottom and pop up unexpectedly in front of the goal. In our case we are going to learn to retain the breath for a far worthier purpose.

1. Here is the first exercise. Practice it every day once or twice for at least two weeks before going on to number 2. Continue it even after this. In fact it is a great invigorator and quite properly could be used by you every day for the rest of your life. It is—as you will see—extremely simple. Its purpose is to expand the lung capacity and help make easier a complete control of your breath. Just do this:

Breathe in to full lung capacity, fill your lungs to the count of 4. Then without pause, exhale to the count of 11. You can see from this that the intake is rapid but the exhalation slow. With a little practice, this should be easy to do. Count as you breathe in and out, always in the same cadence. Repeat this inhalation and exhalation 10 times at a sitting the first week. Then increase it gradually until you are doing it 20 times at a sitting and continue thereafter at that rate. In the first week or so, just seek to gain control—good smooth intake and exhalation are essential. When your control is positive and automatic, and this should be in about two weeks, go on to the next exercise.

2. Continue the breathing as in the foregoing, in for the count of 4, out to the count of 11, but now add a visualization. This means that you are to picture in your mind's eye the following:

Visualize the sun. See the sun as a great white light somewhere above your head. It matters not where it actually is or whether it is day or night. In your visualization see the sun shining brightly above you. Then with each exhalation, as you count to 11, visualize the brilliant white rays of the sun coming down upon you and entering your body through the top of your head and also through your spine in the region of your heart. See this occur only on the exhalation. As you inhale once again, the sun should be shining brightly above you but when you start to exhale see its rays flow down and fill you once again with their divine effulgence.

This is the simple technique for increasing psychic energy by means of directed breath. Don't underrate it. At first only a small amount of psychic energy is collected. But as you proceed, your breathing will become better balanced and your visualization clearer and less confused. This will bring better and better results.

Simple though this appears, it is basic. Adaptations of this technique will be given in later chapters for accomplishing certain definite, highly sophisticated tasks. But you will not be able to call upon and direct the required psychic energy until you have mastered this first lesson and trained your reflexes accordingly. So don't neglect it. And don't imagine you can do it too often. Even ten or twelve repetitions a day are not too many. Every one will help.

USING THE MIND TO INCREASE PSYCHIC ENERGY

In this exercise you are to breathe easily and normally. Better still, forget entirely about your breath and concentrate your entire attention upon the visualization you have selected. There are a great many available. Study well and practice carefully the two I give you here. I am sure that when you have thoroughly explored the possibilities inherent in these mental exercises you will understand the training process and be able to plan other techniques yourself.

1. Select a place where you will not be disturbed for 15 to 20 minutes, seat yourself comfortably and relax. Breathe normally. In fact, the less attention you give your breathing the better. When you are completely quiet turn your attention to your heart. In your mind's eye, see it giving out a pink radiation, like light from a pink-tinted electric bulb, but more brilliant. Hold your attention in your heart for the count of nine. Do not hold your breath but breathe in and out quite normally the entire time.

Now transfer your attention from your heart to the very top of your head and hold it there while you count to 15. As you move your attention from your heart to the crown of your head, carry with it the pink color. Thus, when your attention is focused in this new spot you should see a sphere of brilliant pink light immediately above and interpenetrating your head.

The third and last step is to visualize this pink cloud growing larger and larger so that it gradually envelops your entire body, just as if you were sitting within a brilliant egg-shaped pink cloud. Hold this visualization while you mentally count to 12.

This is the first part. When completed proceed immediately to the second part which is quite similar except for the following changes:

Focus your attention first in your throat in the vicinity of your Adam's apple while you count to 9. Visualize a brilliant blue light emanating from this throat center. As you reach 9 transfer your attention once again to the top of your head and hold it there while you count to 15. These counts should be measured and evenly paced a little slower than the normal heartbeat. Carry to the top of your head the visualization you have of a blue sphere and see it radiating brilliantly as it hovers immediately over your head.

When you reach 15 see this ball of blue light begin to grow larger. See it expand until it is all about you and you are completely bathed in a shining blue cloud. Hold this picture while you count to 12.

This exercise is in three parts and each part has three steps. Here is the third part:

Visualize a great white light radiating out of your forehead from a point between the eyebrows about one inch above the root of the nose. Hold this picture while you count 9 and then transfer your attention once again to the top of your head and see the sphere of brilliant white light resting there as you count to 15. At the count of 15 see the light expand until it becomes a great white cloud which completely envelops you. Then hold this visualization for 12 counts as before.

This completes the exercise. When you have finished sit quietly for a few moments. You have started great forces in motion and, even though you may at first be conscious of no change, it is wise *to let them develop their own momentum* before disturbing your psychic recovery with the banalities of the workaday world. It will not be too long before you see the wisdom in this. Then you will happily sit in quiet for as long as time permits and consciously drink in the psychic energies as they flow into your being.

2. The second exercise employs not only the mind but also the will. In fact all conscious gathering of psychic energy employs will, usually as a control on mental or physical activity. But in this exercise the will is applied directly to the energy itself.

There are two ways to perform this exercise. The exercise is the same, it brings the same faculties into play and should give the same results regardless of which form is used. The forms differ only in the visualization employed.

Form I.

Visualize yourself surrounded by cold. This may be air, ice, water or snow. It makes no difference. But it must be cold and, what is most important, you must feel this cold. This will require an effort of will. It is not necessary, nor should you even try, to find a genuinely cold place. It may be 70°, or 90°, or 40° where you are. The physical conditions are to be ignored. You are going to create your own atmosphere.

So by an effort of will—and it will require a vigorous effort—visualize yourself completely immersed in cold. Feel the cold so keenly you have a tendency to shiver. Keep making it colder. Then, when it is so cold you can hardly stand it, reverse the process and start to generate heat. If your visualization of cold has been good, your skin will actually feel cold, your whole body will be cold. So your warming up process will be genuine. It is the same as the cold visualization but this time you must overcome the cold and generate enough heat to make you feel hot—to actually perspire. You do this by visualizing the heat as starting internally in the vicinity of your solar plexus. The small warm spot should grow under the demand of your will until it is almost like an electric furnace radiating heat in all directions particularly to your body's extremities. As this heat grows it will cause vibratory ripples to extend outward from the center, each one a little stronger and a little warmer than the one previous. When you are no longer cold, but indeed quite hot, the exercise is finished. In its entirety from normal to cold to hot and back to normal it should not take more than 15 minutes at first. When you have become skilled it can be done in less than 5.

Form II.

As I have indicated, this is but a different visualization from form I. The purpose and result are the same, the means are approximately the same and only the visualization and the corresponding effort of will are different.

With this exercise visualize first a sphere of light about 6 feet immediately above your head. The sphere should appear like a brilliant white cloud 4 or 5 feet across. When this sphere is quite visible in your mind's eye, use your will to attempt to lift your body off the chair and up into the center of the sphere. This is not entirely impossible but you are not likely to achieve it at first try. Nor even after a good many tries, so don't worry about the physical part. The key element here is the effort you put forth to raise yourself. When you do this you subconsciously demand psychic energy. You actually draw it into you by the action of your will.

Since at first this may present quite a struggle, stop after 10 minutes of trying. Remember it is not of the greatest importance that you actually lift yourself up in a physical sense. The critical factor is the demand you make for the energy to do this and the subsequent extra supply that comes to you.

It may happen—and eventually it will happen—that as you mentally strive to raise yourself up to the sphere of light above you, you find yourself moving upward and into the sphere. This will not be a physical movement—at least that is not likely. But it will be an actual raising up of the vibrations in your being which will translate itself to your conscious mind as an ascension. Interestingly enough, after such an experience your physical body will actually feel lighter, a condition which will usually prevail for two or three hours.

The foregoing information and exercises will enable you to add substantially to your normal supply of psychic energy, but only if you follow the suggestions given and practice the exercises. A sword that is never taken from the scabbard accomplishes nothing. You have within you the power to do great things but it is necessary to bring it out and use it. And even a small effort will show amazing results.

This chapter has been devoted to the basics, the foundation of knowledge and skills upon which your success must be built. In the next chapter and those that follow I will tell you how to apply psychic energy to achieve the results you desire.

3

The Gift of Prophecy and How
You May Power It With
Psychic Energy

As the Bible relates, Saul of Tarsus, also known as St. Paul the Apostle, was a Roman citizen of Jewish faith who had been brought up and educated in Tarsus in Cilicia. He was a man of great integrity and up to the turning point in his life, which occurred on the road to Damascus, his conduct had been dominated by strict adherence to the written law.

This is not a digression, as will presently become clear. For it was while on the way to Damascus, to punish those whom he considered lawbreakers and blasphemers, that Paul experienced a breakthrough into a higher level of consciousness. He had always possessed psychic energy. His relatively blameless life and his high resolve to follow the law and serve his God acted as an accumulator of vast amounts of this fiery force. But because he did not understand the energy at his command he made no attempt to use it until its pressure on his mind became so great that it broke through into an expanded awareness.

49

HOW ST. PAUL WAS CHANGED BY PSYCHIC ENERGY

In an instant Paul became conscious on the second level, the level above the physical. Its sudden appearance struck his vision as a great light which temporarily blinded him. Only very seldom is a person elevated in an instant from physical to psychic awareness. Usually this process is quite gradual. One first sees little flashes of light, "stars" they are called, when a truth is spoken or when a new idea strikes. These are gone in an instant, a fraction of a second. Later, usually when at ease with the eyes closed, a broader flash of brilliant light will appear, light very much like the brightest sunlight. This too lasts but an instant, but when it is repeated it lingers a little longer each time. Thus does the student working with psychic energy gradually develop his inner vision.

After his "illumination," as it is called, Paul's whole life was changed. He saw things differently and understood far better the mysteries of our existence. These he tried to explain to others but found it difficult to convey such new and strange ideas to minds that were not yet ready. He preached sermons, he gave classes and he wrote letters to his students and followers. Those letters that have been preserved are known as the epistles of St. Paul.

In writing to his students at Corinth (Corinthians I, Chapter 12, V. 7-11) Paul describes some of the gifts of psychic energy. Remember it was necessary for him to use words which could awaken an understanding response in the minds of pupils whose consciousness was not nearly so developed as the average man's is today. So he called psychic energy the gift of the Spirit. Here are his words:

7. But the manifestation of the Spirit is given to every man to profit withal.

8. For to one is given the Spirit of the word of wisdom; to another the word of knowledge by the same Spirit;

9. To another faith by the same Spirit; to another the gifts of healing by the same Spirit;

10. To another the working of miracles; to another prophecy;

to another discerning of spirits; to another diverse kinds of tongues; to another interpretation of tongues.

11. But all these worketh that one and the selfsame Spirit, dividing to every man severally as he will.

Thus wrote a man of honor, a man of probity, nearly two thousand years ago. He said "The manifestation of the Spirit (psychic energy) is given to every man to profit withal." Can any statement be clearer? This obviously means that everyone possesses psychic energy but it rests with the individual to determine how and to what extent he will use it. Then Paul goes further. He says that it lies within the power of the average human to acquire certain unusual abilities by employing psychic energy. He enumerates the working of miracles, the healing of the injured and sick, the discerning of spirits and the gift of prophecy among others. Our study of psychic energy will examine each of these gifts. In this chapter we will analyze prophecy and describe how you may achieve the ability to look into the future.

A PROPHECY FOR THE NEAR FUTURE

There is today a widespread fear that an atomic war may be triggered and the human race decimated in the subsequent holocaust. The bombs are certainly there ready to be used, and in the face of present human and national instability this seems a reasonable possibility. But I will say now that such a war will not occur.

If you have such fears, allay them. I do not offer assurance of immediate peace. On the contrary, nations will be fussing with each other, threatening, bickering and generally acting like spoiled children for several decades to come. But atomic war and the wholesale desolation it implies is no longer in the realm of probability.

Such wholesale slaughter is not considered necessary or advisable and there have been forces released to prevent it. Some evidence of this is already apparent. The young people, the teenagers in all countries, have such a horror of war that they are publicly protesting it in every way open to them. As more and more are added to their ranks and their demands are made with increasing insistence, the executive heads of these countries will be forced to weigh all decisions and actions on the scale with this new and dynamic expression of public opinion.

Gradually it will become apparent that open armed conflict is abhorred by most people and that few condone it. In certain extremely pugnacious nations, where police controls prevent the voice of the people from being heard, there will arise such rebellion and internal strife that all thoughts of international aggression will be set aside. The result will be a continuation of the present armed truce until more reasonable solutions are found.

If this seems to be prophecy—so be it.

THE NATURE OF PROPHECY

Foreknowledge of any event is given the general term *precognition* which means to know in advance. There are many levels of pre-cognition. You may know you are going to attend the theatre tonight because you have planned to go and have already purchased the tickets. Of course many things might happen to change this, but in general it may be said you have a foreknowledge of this event because you yourself have planned it.

This is one type of pre-cognition, foreknowledge based on your own planning. There is a related pre-cognition which is based upon foreknowledge of another's plans. These plans may be told you by their originator, you may read about them, hear about them or learn about them in some other way. You may even tune in telepathically on the thinking of the planner. But these and several other kinds of foreknowledge will not be considered here. For example, we confidently expect it to be cold next winter and warm next summer. All recurring phenomena such as day and night, winter and summer, the moon cycles, vegetation changes and so on have been so observed and categorized, and similar groupings can be predicted with almost mathematical certainty. This is pre-cognition, to be sure, but it is not what we know as prophecy.

HOW PROPHECY WORKS

The accepted definition of prophecy is to predict in advance an occurrence which cannot be known or anticipated from information normally available. A dictionary gives a somewhat oversimplified version, "To predict or foretell, especially under divine inspiration." Those people present and past who have accurately foretold events are human beings like ourselves. They have employed equipment which cannot be too different from our own. To say that they were "divinely inspired" may be true in a very broad sense but this does not really explain what has taken place. In order to get closer to actual facts and to make this clearer, let us examine the mechanics of prophecy and see how it works.

An oft-repeated analogy is the man on the roof of a tall building located at the intersection of two highways. He can see in all four directions but the traffic on each highway can only see along the highway on which it travels. The man observes two cars traveling at a high speed approaching the intersection at right angles to each other. Each driver is unaware of the danger that threatens, but the man above can predict with a fair degree of accuracy that there will be an accident. He is in possession of information not available to the car drivers. Therefore his prediction, while a calculated judgment for him, is prophetic for the drivers.

This is the way all prophecy works. The more information you have, the more accurate will be your prediction. As you get higher above the event itself—not in altitude but in awareness of probable influences—more and more factors will disclose themselves. Thus a man imbued with a great amount of psychic energy who has raised his consciousness to, let us say, the third level will be able to foretell most events two or three years in advance, and some events even farther into the future.

In order to clear up an important point let us go back to the man on the roof who has predicted an accident. There is always the possibility that caution may strike one of the drivers and lead him to apply the brakes as he nears the intersection. This, of course, will prevent the accident and render false the prediction of the man on the building. This can happen to any prophecy. Human decision may change the course of every event. Remember this. Many prophecies come true. Many others offered in just as good faith do not. Human decision is the unpredictable factor.

ANCIENT PROPHETS

Many holy men of old were referred to as prophets. And they were. Each through training and asceticism had built up in himself great stores of psychic energy which enabled him to raise his consciousness to the level of causes. There the myriad causes affecting future events may be observed and the results calculated. Some of the enlightened men were aware of the technique they employed, others used it unconsciously. It is the same today.

TODAY'S PROPHETS

Prophecy is not a lost art. We have our prophets and some have achieved a high record of accuracy, and about the best known in this country today is Jeane Dixon of Washington, D.C. Books have been written about her; she has a syndicated daily newspaper column; at periodic intervals she makes forecasts on a great many topics of national and international interest which are then published in magazines and newspapers; and she is always in demand for radio and television appearances. In an interview published in *Parade Magazine* in 1956, Jeane Dixon stated that the 1960 election would be dominated by labor and won by a Democrat. "He will be assassinated or die in office but not necessarily in the first term ' she said at that time.

Thus she foretold the election of John F. Kennedy to the presidency and his subsequent assassination. She has made hundreds of other prophecies. Prominent among those that have been confirmed are the untimely deaths of Dag Hammarskjold and of Justice Frank Murphy, the success of the Russians in space and the time of Franklin Roosevelt's death. Her prophecies have not always come true but she has a high record of accuracy. She explains it to herself in the language of St. Thomas Aquinas, the great theologian of the Catholic Church, who said there are two kinds of prophecy, that given by God in a vision which is inflexible and that obtained in some other way which is subject to changing conditions not anticipated at the time the prophecy is given. She says the prophecy of the assassination of Jack Kennedy was given in a vision and was therefore unchangeable but that most of her other forecasts have been of the second order. Included in this second category was the trouble in California she forecast for Robert Kennedy and the implication is that his assassination might have been avoided or prevented.

Another very accurate prophet of the present century was Edgar Cayce who died in 1945. Cayce's prophecies were always given in connection with, or as correlative to, some other information that had been requested of him. He did not like to predict, believing it had a bad effect on people. But he did make certain very dramatic statements regarding the future as follows:

1. The earth will be broken up in the western portion of America.
2. A large portion of Japan will go into the sea.
3. The upper portion of Europe will be changed.
4. New land will appear off the east coast of America probably in 1968 or 1969 and some remains of an Atlantis civilization found there.
5. The lower part of Manhattan, the island nucleus of New York City, will be destroyed and all of the island severely damaged
6. The Great Lakes will empty into the Gulf of Mexico instead of into the Atlantic via the St. Lawrence River.

Each one of these surprising predictions will be examined and discussed later in this chapter.

More than 400 years ago Nostradamus forecast forty years of famine and drought to occur near the end of the twentieth century. Modern scientists now agree that if the present population explosion continues, the world will have seven billion people about the year 2000 and only food enough for five billion. I think this is a pessimistic assessment of human resourcefulness but at the same time the recommendations these scientists have made must be regarded as wise. They urge the entire world to take the following steps:

1. Establish mandatory birth control on a worldwide basis.
2. Seek new methods of food processing from available oils, vegetables and minerals.
3. Explore the food potential of the sea and create nourishing products from its plankton and algae.
4. Establish large scale conversion plants to change sea water to fresh drinking water.

If the foregoing recommendations are adopted the prophecy of Nostradamus and the predictions of our scientists will prove to be false. Sometimes this is the purpose of prophecy—to warn people to adopt new and different courses of action in order to avoid impending disaster.

There are astrological predictions which concur with Edgar Cayce's forecasts of geological changes. These state that much of California, New York and other parts of our coastline will suffer from upheavals, lands will rise in the Caribbean and the Great Lakes will shift their flow southward. In evaluating these it is important to remember that the astrologer reads only influences from his charts. The interpretations are his own and unquestionably they are guided by what he has heard and read plus whatever personal disposition may be his. It is for this reason that there are so few good astrologers. Good, original interpretive predictions require powerful intuition and great psychic sensitivity. As you can imagine, these qualities are rare.

Another man with prophetic gifts who came into prominence in 1968 is Daniel Logan. He, like Edgar Cayce, bases his forecasts on information obtained on the second level of consciousness, the next level above physical waking awareness. The predictions he has made for individuals have been accurate. This is chiefly because the personality of the individual is present and evident at the sitting along with a host of other palpable influences present and past. In many cases 95 percent of all possible determining causes can be observed and thus fairly accurate predictions made.

It is not possible to make such accurate forecasts where large numbers of people are involved. The number of determining factors, a billion or more in the case of a single individual, is multiplied by geometrical progression with every new person that is added to the group. Even the greatest minds, both in and out of material existence, have difficulty in forecasting national or worldwide occurrences. The end result may be obvious, but the sequence of events leading to it and their timing is so subject to a myriad of human decisions that in most cases only an approximation can be offered.

To minds of those operating on the second level, as did Edgar Cayce in his trances and as does Daniel Logan today in similar trance states, the future is presented as a rule in picture form and is thus accepted by them as an established fact. These pictures are but the impact of thoughtforms created on a higher level on the so-called "astral light" of the second level. Thus when Daniel Logan reports in a trance state that

1. There will be a major war in the 1980's, or
2. Earthquakes will strike not only the west coast but also the east coast of America, or
3. The war in Vietnam and Southeast Asia will continue for many years and even though a break, a temporary peace, may come, it will be resumed once again,

he is relaying information obtained on the second level. There is probably very little question but that there will be damaging earthquakes on the west coast and in the east as well, but the time and the extent of these is not at all definite. There is also possibility of a major war. This is an ever-present sword over our heads. This prediction is nothing more than what 75 percent of the people in the world think and expect. Yet it need not come true. Like the famine and drought prediction of Nostradamus, it can be prevented by timely human decision and action.

Edgar Cayce's prophecies have been given worldwide publicity and are thus known to a great many people. So let us examine those previously enumerated and see if it is possible to find a few rays of sunshine in the gloom. Cayce was primarily interested in helping human beings. In his trance states he diagnosed illnesses, gave medical advice, and suggested lines of activity which would help the questioner live a better and more productive life. He did great work and his unselfish efforts helped thousands. It was only in the course of giving advice in answer to a specific question that references to certain geological changes crept into his replies.

It must be remembered that in almost every "reading" quoted, Cayce's attention was centered upon an individual and his or her personal problems. His field of observation was largely concerned with the millions of possible causes hovering over that particular person. The physical elements impending or already in existence in the body were quite clear. Thus a completely accurate diagnosis of the physical or emotional conditions could be made and alleviating treatment recommended. The amazing success of these treatments wherever they were employed (not everyone had the good sense to do what was recommended) had given Cayce a reputation for infallibility. And he was very nearly infallible in his diagnosis of conditions already in physical existence. But unfortunately many are willing to credit that same infallibility to his statements about the future. This is not good judgment, and if he were to testify he would be the first to tell you so.

Each person carries with him not only the evidence of his own future but also that of his contribution, small or large, to the group to which he belongs. Thus in treating an individual, Cayce became aware of that person's contribution to the future of his family, nation and race. But because his attention was centered upon that individual, this contribution (like the foreground of a photograph) was enlarged out of its true relation to the whole. To use a rather trite phrasing, he saw the future through the aura of the individual before him. To a greater or lesser degree this is true of all prophetic utterance. A holy man in Greece will see the future as it affects his country and will enlarge out of proportion the Greek influence on the world as a whole. This is not patriotism but a perfectly natural tendency to accord greater importance to the nearby and familiar. The death of the boy next door is more moving than that of an unknown child in Biafra.

Most precognition occurs when the observer gets far enough above the event that the majority of factors bearing upon it can be observed and correlated. The conscious mind is unable to do this but the inner mind can evaluate all of these diverse elements and with computer-like speed and accuracy reach the most probable conclusion. The higher the observer can get, the greater will be the number of influencing factors that come under his observation. The word "higher" here does not mean geographical altitude but the higher vibratory realm which is extremely difficult to reach in the waking state. (Cayce and Logan found best results in a trance state. Jeane Dixon usually releases her subconscious by gazing into a crystal ball.) In this "higher" state the subconscious mind observes energies and forces and calculates the probable result of their confluence. This conclusion usually presents itself to the conscious mind in picture form. Sometimes all of the observed factors click precisely into place and the event occurs

THE GIFT OF PROPHECY

as foreseen. Sometimes human decision will change one or more elements and the prophecy becomes false. There are some great minds far more capable of prophecy than are we average humans, yet one of them has said that "the walls of Hierarchy are covered with false prophecies." The whimsical changes in the human mind are, on a large scale, almost impossible for even the greatest minds to predict.

At this point it might be well to discuss the prophecies offered by the guides and discarnate advisors of spiritualists. This is not to be construed as an attempt to evaluate the work of spiritualists and the Spiritualist Church and certainly there is no intention to deprecate it. However it is important to see clearly the elements that comprise the prophecies which are offered in this way.

It is normal for a person who has become convinced a departed loved one is communicating with him to give great credence to all that is said. Once the initial skepticism is broken down by the evidence of the intimate detail offered, then all else is usually accepted without question. Yet the discarnate entity, whether he present himself as Uncle Joe or the spirit of Abraham Lincoln, is no better equipped to judge the progress of events in his present state than he was in a physical body. True he has access to more information, he can see more causes, but his appraisal of these causes and the conclusions he reaches will be no better than yours or mine in the same situation. They try to help but there are many factors, particularly the time element, which are beyond their capacity to evaluate.

Sometimes those who have the welfare of the human race at heart view a certain possibility and, deciding it is undesirable, take steps to prevent its occurrence. Human free will is never curtailed but there is no reason why certain lines of conduct should not be made to appear more attractive than others. (Do not our advertisers do this daily?) For example, more than three hundred years ago, the San Andreas fault was observed and its future potential for destruction appraised. At that time a highly sensitive man, a Catholic priest, Fra Junipero Serra, was sent to the area. The religious order which sent him was not aware of the far-reaching extent of his mission nor could they have understood had it been told to them. To them, it merely seemed like a good idea at the time. Father Serra founded missions all through the western and southern parts of California, most of them on the line of the San Andreas fault or west of it. These missions, some still active and others abandoned, are in the nature of great magnets which have subtly drawn high-minded and spiritual people to that area. You have heard it said that every strange and odd cult exists in California. This is true but there are also many fine and worthwhile groups with headquarters there. All of these people, both the solid and reliable and those of a more frivolous nature, have one thing in common. They are all people of good will. They all have good hearts and high intentions.

Thus among the millions who today live west of the San Andreas fault, there is a great leavening of love and good will. True, there are many who have low tendencies but the evil thoughts they radiate are absorbed and minimized by the good intentions of the majority. What might have become a modern Sodom and suffered a similar cataclysmic destruction will be spared to a large degree because the thinking of a great number of people there has lightened and lifted the pressure.

Analysis of the Cayce predictions

This brings us to a consideration of the Cayce predictions which are listed earlier in this chapter.

1. "The earth will be broken up in the western portion of America." There will be earthquakes, bad ones. All geophysicists say the pressure is building along the San Andreas fault and when the tension forces an eruption there will be destruction. But the land to the west of the fault will not break off and slide into the Pacific carrying millions to their deaths. At least it will not occur in this age which still has a long way to go. It is not possible today for us to estimate the extent of the damage the quakes will cause and where the worst will occur. Sometime in the next few years, maybe ten to fifteen years, the fault will slip and earthquakes occur at several points along its length. There will be loss of life and destruction of property. But it will only be a fraction of the holocaust which is forecast. Thus can the human spirit change the course of events.

2. "A large portion of Japan will go into the sea." At the time this prophecy was made, World War II had not yet started. Since then

the Japanese people have suffered greatly and have been led to a new outlook on world affairs. If this continues, and it probably will, Japan like western California will be but lightly struck and the heaviest blows avoided.

3. "The upper portion of Europe will be changed." From a political point of view, this has already taken place. Much will depend now on how the dominated nations and their people act in the next ten years. The growth of the common market leading to a much smoother inter-relationship is most encouraging. If this continues as it has started, most large scale geological changes will be deferred to a future age.

4. "New land will appear on the east coast of America." Some evidence of this is already apparent. In February 1968, the *Palm Beach Post* carried the story of a "find" of archaeological significance off the coast of the Grand Bahama Island between it and the Florida mainland. Outlines of the ruins of walls and other building structures were discerned in 90 feet of water. An expedition was formed to explore this unusual find but since then no further word has been given out. In the 1960 report in connection with the International Geophysical Year (I. G. Y.) statements were included to the effect that underwater land has been observed rising in the Caribbean area in some places more than 1000 feet since previous soundings. There is every likelihood there will be more news on this in the near future.

5. "The lower part of Manhattan and maybe the whole island will be destroyed." This is definitely possible. There is a fault, a crack in the primal rock base, which starts at the East River, near 14th Street, and angles in a northwesterly direction to the Hudson River, near 40th Street. All major building contractors now know this and are reluctant to construct tall buildings along it. However, the land to the north and south has been considered safe and is heavily built up. It will not take much additional tension to move the land along this fault. When this occurs there could be a shifting of all the land in Manhattan south of it, and resulting great destruction. This could happen within 30 years or possibly not for 130 years. Edgar Cayce once dreamed he visited a destroyed city in the year 2100 and was told by workmen there that it was New York. But then this was a dream.

6. "The Great Lakes will empty into the Gulf of Mexico." The general concept in this prophecy is that the land in the Central States will tilt so that the water in the Great Lakes will change its flow to a southerly direction. This may eventually occur but not in the foreseeable future. However, there is presently in use an inland waterway

from Lake Michigan to the Mississippi River which makes it possible for cargo steamers to move from the Great Lakes to the Gulf of Mexico, a partial confirmation of the prediction.

In considering prophecies, particularly dismal ones, we should recall that those involving large numbers of people rarely occur in the manner and to the extent described by the prophet. These prophets are human beings. They see certain events on the screen of their consciousness but always through the film created and colored by their emotions, understanding and previous experience. Often when projected into reality the vision of a destroyed city becomes a riot-torn town like Watts, bad enough in itself but only a fraction of the devastation prophesied, a charging rhinoceros becomes a yapping dog, and the end of an age may mean only that a new and better one has started.

HOW YOU MAY DEVELOP PROPHETIC ABILITY

Nearly everyone has some degree of precognitive ability. Sometimes this may display itself as apprehension, sometimes as a hunch, and sometimes as joyful anticipation when you feel certain "something nice" is going to happen. These impressions cannot as a rule be predicted in advance. They come only occasionally and usually without any preliminary warning. Thus we seldom act on them and become aware of them only in retrospect. You can sharpen this innate capacity by the proper understanding of psychic energy and its intelligent use. In order that you may comprehend the hows, whens and whys of prophecy, and "gifts of the spirit," it is necessary to first know something of the mechanics of awareness.

THE MECHANICS OF AWARENESS

There are four levels of human awareness. This can be likened to a four-storied dwelling with stairways and elevators running from floor to floor. Nearly everyone lives on the ground floor or level number one. Some are crowded ten or more to a room in which all see, hear and think the same things. Others have private apartments which they may share with one or two, while a few have very large expanses in which they usually live alone.

Those with the large apartments are aware of far more than those who are crowded together. Each room of theirs has a different view and contains varied facilities for acquiring and storing knowledge. But all of this knowledge, all of these observations, are on the level where they live, the first level, the physical level. Thus there are many grades and depths of awareness on this the physical level, as is true of every other level.

The next higher level of awareness has been called by many names. These are not significant. They are but the endeavors of those who know to convey information to those who do not know. To designate it as the second level is descriptive enough. Anyone on the first level can get to the second level by climbing one of the stairways, which are numerous and for the most part conveniently located. All that is necessary is to know that the stairway is there, that to climb it is rewarding, and then make the effort to do so. There are also elevators, but these are few and their operators permit entry only to those who have qualified. The reason for this apparent selectivity is that an elevator may take you in an instant not only to the second level but also to the third or fourth and this might be a devastating experience without due preparation. Not everyone has as solid a purity of motive as Saul of Tarsus. The view on the second level is far greater and much more can be observed. Also there is less crowding and each individual has a much wider range of uninhibited awareness than on the physical level. Observers on this level are usually so impressed with the clarity and distance of their vision there, they are prone to believe they are witnessing all there is to be seen. This, of course, is not so. For there are two higher levels, each with 1000 times the perspective of the level below. On this second level may be observed the causes leading to events and other manifestations on the physical level below. Thus when you raise your consciousness to the second level you will find it possible to predict certain events with a fair degree of certainty. We will come back to this.

The third level is that of ideas, of the inspirations that move great composers and artists, that guide writers and inventors. To the mind that reaches this level, beauty and order are the paramount considerations and only incidentally does prevision occur.

But when it does, it is much more accurate because the range of observation is far, far greater than that on the level below, the second level. Nearly everyone reaches the second level for a longer or shorter period from time to time, but only a very few ever reach the third level. Vast areas of knowledge are available here and it is only the limitation of the physical brain that prevents those who contact the third level from bringing more than a thimbleful back. It is almost like trying to carry water in your fist. The tighter you grasp it, the less you can bring with you.

The fourth level is that of the spirit. Only a handful in each age ever reach it. It is the fountainhead of psychic energy, the great power that with intelligent development enables you to raise your consciousness to ever higher levels, to the second and, yes, even to the third if you are so focussed. But now, since it is the purpose of this work to help you expand your consciousness, we will return to a consideration of the second level and how you may learn to enter it at will.

We earlier referred to stairways. These are many and each is different. You may go up one, I another. But all have this in common: An effort must be made, energy must be employed. Psychic energy must be assembled, accumulated, and then directed by the will. This is accomplished by visualization. Here is a technique that works.

1. Demand psychic energy. Visualize vast streams of pure white radiance streaming into your being from above. Want this energy, demand it with all your will, feel love for it, then see it and realize it as it tingles through you, an accomplished fact.

2. After a short pause, visualize your whole being lifted up into a brilliant clear white light. See it like an envelope all around you. Feel its vibrant quality tingle on your skin. Let its invigorating freshness envelop and nourish you.

That is the exercise. Now for some explanations. In the beginning, attempt this only when alone and in a relaxed position. Seat yourself in a large comfortable chair or lie flat on a couch or bed.

The willful invoking of energy should not be continued for more than a minute. The following visualization can then be carried for four or five minutes.

When first performed it is quite likely that no immediate result will be observed. There will be an effect but the normal awareness of the average person is not sufficiently keen to detect it. It is only after repeated regular practice that the impression becomes cumulatively more potent. This in turn makes you more sensitive.

A good place to practice this exercise is in bed, either just after retiring or in the morning just before rising. If performed in the evening just before falling asleep, you will have interesting dreams. Try to remember them. It is best if you write what you remember immediately on waking because these memories are fleeting and will probably be gone in an hour or two. Much of what you experience in these dreams will be prophetic in nature. Usually these pre-cognitions will be of quite trivial incidents. Write them down anyway and when you find them coming true this will give you confidence and encourage you to additional effort.

In the morning, try to maintain that drowsy, half-awake attitude usually experienced on waking. From this state the second level can be easily reached.

THE SECOND LEVEL

There will come a time when your persistence will be rewarded, sooner for some than for others. The light you visualize about you will suddenly become real, much brighter than your best imagining. The air will have a clarity never before observed, and your entire being will be filled with vigor and will feel much lighter. You will have reached the second level.

The unfamiliar brightness will probably startle you into wakefulness back on the physical level in your first few attempts but if you repeat your efforts you will soon find the experience most pleasant. It is then that you will gradually become aware that there is more than light around you. Depending upon your interest, various events will appear before you, unreeling themselves somewhat in the nature of a colored motion picture which is all around you giving the impression that you, the observer, are actually in the midst of an event while it is taking place. This is but one type of hundreds of different exposures to causes. At another time you may see the actions of a person you know, see not only what he does (or will do) in the future but all of the causes in the past that have led him to this course of action. This will give you a much better understanding of people and their motives which will result in a compassionate attitude toward their weaknesses and errors.

As you become more familiar with these new surroundings your awareness will continue to expand. There may come a time when you will believe you have at your beck and call all of the world's knowledge and much that is beyond. But this will not be true. The possibility of acquiring it will be there, but you will still be you. Let me ask you, how much physical knowledge do you presently possess? Do you know all there is to know? Do you think you might have all the physical knowledge that exists in human minds if you could have it just for the asking? Think about this and if you are honest with yourself you will realize that no matter how easy it might be for you to get knowledge you would never have a very large percentage of the total because of several reasons. You might sum these up as follows:

1. Too much trouble and requires too much effort.
2. Not enough interest.
3. Much knowledge is limited by preconceived notions and ideas which prevent its acceptance.
4. Emotional reactions to certain information exist which either distort understanding of it or cause its rejection.

There are others which you can think of but the foregoing are enough to prove the point—you can only gain a fraction of the information available on the second level because you are limited by a human brain with many human prejudices and built-in emotional blocks. These can be smoothed out and eliminated but since you have been acquiring them for a half million years this is no small task and will take a little time in the doing.

The instructions in this and other chapters will, if followed, help you greatly to a purer, clearer line of thought and action. The part devoted later to projection will clarify further the various levels and aid you in your efforts to dwell thereon. The techniques are given here. The decision to use them must be yours.

Because we have touched briefly on the third level of awareness in this chapter we will next consider inspiration which finds its source on that level.

4

How Great Writers, Composers, Artists and Inventors Employ Psychic Energy to Gain Inspiration

Nearly every genius is fully aware that when working under inspiration, direction comes from a source superior to and different from intellect. Not all understand this. Some lesser heroes accept inspiration blindly, joyfully and without question. But the truly great, like Shakespeare, Milton and Wagner, consciously wooed the muse. They understood the source of their inspiration and its dependence upon psychic energy. This energy they cultivated and employed to raise the level of their awareness to the heights of beauty and knowledge.

CARLYLE'S DEFINITION OF GENIUS

Carlyle, in his *Life of Frederick the Great,* defined genius as the "infinite capacity for taking pains." Because every work of genius requires perfection down to the smallest detail, this definition has become quite generally accepted—but not by men of genius. Johannes Brahms, for one, vigorously disagreed. He said at one time that if this definition were true "any patient, plodding mediocrity could become a Bach or a Beethoven."

When his questioner, the eminent violinist Joseph Joachim, pressed him for his own definition, Brahms said, "The real genius draws on an infinite source of wisdom and power. Some who are religiously inclined, call it communing with God. Haydn, for example, put on his best clothes when he was about to compose and made quite a ceremony of it. Others like Wagner and Bach had a clearer understanding and employed a planned technique to reach inspired heights."

BRAHMS UNDERSTOOD PSYCHIC ENERGY

Brahms's guarded words are clear to anyone who understands psychic energy. The words and writings of many men and women of genius reveal that they recognized the source of their inspiration to be closely related to an influx of higher energy and often they used certain exercises to stimulate this energy. Almost the last words written by Shakespeare were

> Now my charms are all o'erthrown
> And what strength I have is mine own
> Which is most faint.

This is an unmistakable statement to the effect that, growing older, he could no longer command as much high energy as heretofore and regarded his normal equipment unequal to the high standard he had established.

Milton's more obscure reference in Book IX of *Paradise Lost* becomes clearer if we understand that he employed psychic energy to create a semi-trance or borderline state between sleeping and full wakefulness, and in this condition found it possible to raise his consciousness to the level of inspired thought. His words are

> If answerable style I can obtain
> Of my celestial patroness who deigns
> Her nightly visitations unimplored,
> And dictates to slumbering or inspires
> Easy my unpremeditated verse.

Two or three hundred years ago it was dangerous to admit any knowledge not embraced by the generally accepted religious framework. Men and women were burned at the stake for such confessions. But as we come nearer to the present day, more definite statements can be found.

One evening, Johannes Brahms, in discussing the famous "Devil's Trill Sonata," said of its composer Tartini, "I learned a valuable lesson from Tartini, that is, never to completely lose consciousness when inducing the semi-trance state. When preparing myself to enter the dream-like state, I often look at the cartoon-like picture of the Devil playing to Tartini which is on the cover of the score in order not to make the same mistake."

He meant, of course, that he wanted to avoid sound sleep and the uncontrolled dreaming that often accompanies deep slumber. This is what had happened to Tartini. His sought for contact with the stream of inspiration was successfully made but, losing conscious control, Tartini dreamed that the Devil had visited his bed-chamber and played a most beautiful violin melody. He brought a clear remembrance of this melody back to waking awareness but cloaked it in the superstitious fantasy of the day when any experience beyond the physical was presumed to have been a visitation of God, Angel or Devil.

INFLUENCE OF RELIGIOUS THOUGHT

Religious thoughtforms were very powerful right up to the present century and every event out of the ordinary was usually explained or understood in orthodox terms. The composer Haydn was convinced that only a personal contact with God enabled him to write great music. He was right, of course, in the sense that it was necessary for him to raise his consciousness up from the ordinary mundane level in order to reach the higher stream of great inspiration. In this he differed from Tartini only in interpretation. Both contacted the same high current but one translated it as communion with God and the other as contact with the Devil.

Brahms, though, saw this much more realistically and so did Richard Strauss who one day said to Arthur Abell who was then European correspondent for the *Musical Courier*, "In my most inspired moods, I have clear-cut and compelling visions involving a higher selfhood. At such moments I feel I am tapping the source of infinite energy."

PSYCHIC ENERGY AIDS INSPIRATION

This is the same sensation one gets when successfully drawing upon psychic energy, a technique which I am teaching you. This great energy has a way of speeding up and helping along all of the projects to which you dedicate yourself. But it is no cure-all. There are definite limitations. It will help a trained musician write a symphony but will give him little or no guidance should he attempt to plead a case in a court of law. On the other hand a trained trial lawyer may become, with its support, a brilliant courtroom virtuoso but will make little progress with a violin. The high-grade, stimulating energy is there and available but it flows best through channels which are already well marked. When you apply it you will reach a higher level of consciousness but this greater awareness will confine itself chiefly to the discipline in which your aptitude and training enable you to best express yourself.

If you are a writer you can write more smoothly and colorfully when you employ psychic energy. And at times, under favorable conditions, high-grade inspiration will stimulate you. If you would court inspiration here is a technique you can employ. There are many, many others, all of them effective. This is one which works for most people.

HOW TO SEEK INSPIRATION

Assemble your writing equipment, paper, typewriter or pencils, references needed and seat yourself at your desk. Then, before starting, sit back relaxed, close your eyes and take six breaths as follows:

1. Breathe in quickly and deeply to the count of four.
2. Hold your breath in to the count of twelve. As you hold your breath visualize a brilliant cloud of shimmering pulsating silver-white radiance two or three feet over your head. This cloud may be small, say two feet in its spherical diameter, or it may be as much as seven or eight feet across.

3. Then breathe out to the count of eight. As you do so, raise your consciousness up and into the center of the cloud so that it contains your head and shoulders within its radiance.

Rhythm plays a part in this exercise, so maintain a steady cadence in your counting. Do not pause between parts 1 and 2 or between 2 and 3, but keep steadily on. When you have finished one cycle of three parts, proceed without pause to the next breath until all six breaths have been completed.

Then set about writing immediately. You may experience a strong desire to doze or to relax a little longer. Do not give in to it but start as quickly as possible to employ the psychic energy you have accumulated. If you have already embarked on a writing project, proceed with what you have been doing. If you have one in mind, start it. If you are still groping for an idea, start writing the first thing that comes to mind. In many cases this will unfold quite naturally as you go along. As you proceed you will find that the longer you write at any one sitting, the more successful your efforts will become. You will thus be encouraged to continue until circumstances or physical fatigue force you to terminate the sitting.

As with any unfamiliar process, practice will be needed before good results are achieved. But after the third or fourth experience you will find yourself writing more rapidly and much more smoothly than ever before. Such is the nature of psychic energy and its power to lift you into a high stream of consciousness.

WELCOME INSPIRATION WHEN IT COMES

This same technique can be employed with profit by composers, artists, architects and engineers. All creative activity can be thus stimulated, if you don't fight it. This last comment may appear gratuitous. It is not. There are many who do not accept inspiration when it comes. Some reject it because of prejudice, some because of limited comprehension, some because of contrary ideas.

This latter problem caused the great inventor, Major E. H. Armstrong, to postpone his greatest gift to broadcasting for many years. In addition to outstanding engineering knowledge, Major Armstrong had imagination, intuition and normally a very open mind. He invented the Armstrong regenerative circuit which permitted the amplification of electrical wave impulses and made possible all broadcasting as we know it today. He has hundreds of other inventions to his credit but in the nineteen-twenties, he, as well as other radio engineers, was stumped by the great problem of static. This is no longer a matter of serious concern. The great power of the transmitting stations and the extreme selectivity of the receiving sets have all but eliminated it. But in the early days of radio broadcasting natural and man-made static frequently provided an unpleasant and undesired background of noise to all radio listening. Armstrong worked for many years to solve this problem. Time and again, the solution came to his mind but he always rejected it before giving it the consideration it deserved. It finally remained for his wife Marian, who was extremely sensitive, to insist he explore the possibilities of frequency modulation as opposed to the then accepted standard method of modulating the amplitude of the carrier wave in the broadcast signal. Thus was FM broadcasting born, some twenty years too late, and it is only in recent years, some thirty odd years after its introduction by Major Armstrong, that it is beginning to gain the recognition it deserves. Yet if Howard Armstrong had accepted his first inspiration and insisted on frequency modulation at a time when either system could have been made standard, all radio broadcasting today would probably be via FM.

Everyone should woo inspiration. People in the creative arts and professions know well that their success depends upon the quality and often the quantity of high-grade product they turn out. For this, blood, sweat and tears are not enough. They must have inspiration and they seek it, often in strange ways. But a mother dealing with small children, a husband with an overworked and high-strung wife, an executive negotiating with workers, all need the inspired direction that comes from the higher mental and emotional contacts made possible through psychic energy.

SOURCES OF INSPIRATION

It is an oversimplification to say that inspiration comes from God or the Cosmic. Of course it does. But so do sunshine and

rainfall and life and spirit and love and enthusiasm and everything else of which we are aware. We can pin-point the origins
of inspiration much closer than that. The simplest is by coming
into mental attunement with one or two other persons who are
working on the same problem or in the same field as you are.
Sometimes both parties are in full possession of all the necessary
knowledge and need only a certain amount of mutual—but not
consciously realized—effort to coordinate this knowledge into
presentable form. A recent example of this was the almost simultaneous submission by two different writers of a magazine article
on exactly the same subject. One writer lived in Maine and the
other in Ohio. They were unknown to each other and had never
met, yet both wrote of the same occurrence that had taken place
in Pennsylvania over 100 years ago.

The story they wrote was based upon information, court records
and such that have been available since the happening. There was
no recent public announcement that might have captured their
attention. Both are professional writers. Both were seeking an
unusual article. Each one independently of the other recalled
hearing something in the past about this crime and each ran it
down in his own way. Yet the stories were written at almost the
same time and about the same incident.

In the broader sense of the word both writers were inspired. But
whether A picked up the idea from B, or B from A will never be
known. There is also the possibility, and a very real one, that both
A and B tuned in on a third party who had the original idea but
never took the time to write it out. This type of "inspiration" is
elementary and occurs quite frequently, sometimes to the em-
barrassment of the parties involved who are suspected of having
copied or stolen from each other.

A second type of inspiration occurs when one tunes in on a
powerful thought form generated in the past by an individual or
group. This is most easily recognized in the work of a writer,
composer or painter, in which case critics say politely if somewhat
cynically that the artist has been "influenced" by the work of
the master who lived many years before. I know of one writer
who feels a close affinity to Lord Byron and believes that Byron's
thoughts influence much of what he writes. But this type of inspiration is also recognized in the political and economic fields.

We have, to date, suffered from the ideas of a long succession of powerful men who were convinced the path to world peace lay through world conquest. None admitted even to themselves that they sought world dominion for self-aggrandizement but proclaimed loudly that world peace was their sole objective. This kind of inspiration we can do without, but it exists!

YOU CAN AND SHOULD SEEK INSPIRATION

The inspiration you should seek comes from a higher source. There is a whole world of wonderful new ideas, melodies, pictures and techniques available to all on the next higher psychic level. It has been called the "rain cloud of knowable things." These are the ideas that are so close to human realization that almost anyone can tap them with but little effort.

Teilhard de Chardin, a man with an illumined mind, proposed in *The Phenomenon of Man*, that we have just now come, along the evolutionary process, to the brink of an enormous expansion in human consciousness. He is right. The development of our awareness is such that we are now ready for these "gifts" as they have been called. But those who will find them first and benefit most are the seekers, the ones like yourself who employ psychic energy to raise their conscious understanding to the slightly higher level where these ideas may be contacted. There one may awaken (so to speak) to that which is on the verge of precipitation into human thinking, life and circumstances. Once the contact has been made and the seeker has been entrusted with this inspiration, he has then the responsibility to handle himself so correctly and wisely that he may become a proper guardian of this treasure and bring it step by step into physical manifestation.

Let me repeat again and emphasize that this ability can be developed by all who read these words. Position, authority, power or skill are not needed. Granted, for some new ideas they are valuable but there are millions of precious drops in this cloud of knowable things and among them are distillations that only you can bring to their fullest efflorescence. There have always been certain men with the ability to draw from on high the ideas and techniques that have led humanity up the path of evolution. Today, the door is opening much wider. In place of a few hundred there are now thousands who, like yourself, may with proper effort tap this beneficent raincloud. Each person who becomes aware of this is urged to act, to do his or her best to bring out this precipitation of new ideas into the consciousness of a world struggling in the anguish of reorganization and regeneration.

Because of its importance I will repeat this again. The cooperation and effort of every awakened person are needed. There is so much to be known, so much to be given, and so few who know how to recognize and use it. Seek out psychic energy. Train yourself and build in a bountiful supply of this precious force. Then raise your consciousness to the highest level of which you are capable and with purity of motive bring back to humanity the treasures that await there.

5

How to Employ Psychic Energy
to Influence Others
to Help You

One of the greatest assets of psychic energy is the power it gives you over others. This power is very real and many people employ it, some consciously, others without clear understanding of the means they have used. How often have you said of a person, "He has a powerful personality," having in mind the ease with which he dominates others and sweeps all opposition aside. Realize now that the power you recognize in him is the product of a flood of psychic energy which you too can command.

One exercises authority in many ways, some direct, others more subtle. But we do not concern ourselves here with vested authority, the voice of the parent to the child, the instruction of the teacher to a class or the command of an officer to his men. Our interest lies with a different level of influence beyond and above physical force or constraint and simple appeals to reason. You have certainly found yourself influenced at one time or another by a friend, a relative or a loved one and quite willingly doing as they wished even when it presented difficulties for yourself. Even when you rebelled you probably chided yourself for being selfish or unreasonable. This acquiescence is natural with the people close to you, those who make up your life. You try to accommodate yourself to their needs and expect them to do the same for you. Usually this influence is benign and well intended but occasionally it can be harmful as in the case when a mother is over-protective toward a grown child or a strong-willed child is too demanding on its parents The energy involved in this interplay is psychic energy. It is the strange fluid that flows between people and permits the development of harmonious relationships. As more and more people seek unselfishly to employ psychic energy in this way, the frictions between them will dissolve and a happier concordance result. This is equally true of nations and races.

There are many ways in which you may use psychic energy to influence others. These range all the way from the simple appeal of a child who turns his big blue eyes toward you as he asks for a second helping of dessert on up to the vast force exerted by a spellbinding orator as he sways an auditorium full of people. However there are three basic techniques which embrace all psychic control whether the effort be consciously or subconsciously motivated. But before embarking on their description and instructions for their employment I must first offer a word of advice.

SEEK FIRST TO SERVE BEFORE DEMANDING SERVICE

Psychic energy is impersonal, like sunlight. By nature it is good, but such is the power of the will of man it may be, and unfortunately occasionally is, put to evil use. By "evil" is here meant a use which brings harm to another. Fortunately most of us have so many built-in safeguards and inhibitions that we find it quite impossible to deliberately and consciously harm another. And it is well for us that this is so, for psychic energy when directed outward has a boomerang effect. It brings back to the sender a multitude of unimagined blessings if his sending is good. This is the meaning of "Cast thy bread upon the waters," etc. But the opposite is also true and an evilly planned influence often brings back tragedy to its creator. Fortunately, it is the rare person who deliberately plans to harm another. But many of us quite often contemplate and wish for certain results which seem good to us at the time without considering that others may be harmed in their realization. It is within the realm of possibility that you may successfully influence a person to act in your favor without being aware that this very action will bring harm to someone else. You must take pains to avoid this for your own benefit. Of course every action has far-reaching consequences and no one can predict just what the distant future may bring. But the possibilities of the immediate present are usually quite clear. So if even the slightest spitefulness or vengefulness or any similar destructive emotion enters your mood, know that your efforts will result in more harm to you than good.

Most people make the mistake of assuming there is only a limited amount of wealth, or power, or happiness in this world and in order to obtain a fair share it is necessary to take it away from someone else. Nothing could be more wrong. The wealth of this world, its joy and happiness, are all unlimited. You can have all you want. You need only create it for yourself. When you try to take it away from another it loses its sweetness and turns to ashes in your mouth. It is most unfortunate that some people who learn about psychic energy and develop the power of influencing others become quite ruthless. For power exerts a corrupting influence which I must warn you about in order that you may guard against it. So it is that at the very beginning of this lesson on how to influence others I give you this warning: "Never use your power to harm anyone or cause that person to bring injury on another." This is for your own good, for the penalties far outweigh the rewards. No one will be there to judge you nor will there be a court of appeal. It is in the nature of the energy itself to correct and rebalance all misapplications and it cannot be deceived. This is what the prophet meant when he said so long ago, "God is not mocked."

Now that this most necessary warning has been given, let us consider the ways in which you can benefit yourself through the proper use of psychic energy. The simplest and most obvious way of winning support for a project close to your heart is by persuasion. There are many types of persuasion—argument, proof, example, reasoning, suggestion and dominance among others. Most of these you understand very well; you probably use them daily. Some are not so familiar and probably the least understood is personality's influence. This last is a subtle but effective technique and the remainder of this chapter will be devoted to explaining it to you and teaching you how and when to employ it.

LEARNING HOW TO EMPLOY PERSONALITY INFLUENCE

At the start it is best to defer thoughts of help for yourself and set out to help another. You will learn more quickly and it is safer too. Do not be impatient about this. Some of the most powerful men of our time began their careers with completely unselfish attempts to help their fellow men and their countries. When Benito Mussolini first began to achieve power his sole aim was to improve his beloved Italy. And in the beginning he did indeed give it a standard of excellence it had never before enjoyed. The streets became clean, the people took pride in their personal appearance and the condition of their homes, the crime rate dropped and even in Naples where many boast of their criminal exploits it was safe for a woman to walk abroad at night unattended. Of course when his power became great, Mussolini suffered its corroding effect. He then began to indulge his vanities and to court power for its own sake. But at first he used his amazing influence over men to help them without much thought for himself.

Franklin Delano Roosevelt was another great man who started his political career with a sincere and honest desire to help his country and its people. He was wealthy. He did not need money and at that time power was not even in sight. As was mentioned in the first chapter Roosevelt employed great psychic energy and his influence on men was most powerful. This was a personality influence. In his presence almost no one could resist him when he chose to turn on his "charm," as it was called. It was even effective over the radio and his talks swayed millions. He was well aware of his influence over others and employed it consciously. A friend of mine, who was later in Truman's Cabinet and who knew Roosevelt personally, spoke to him after his return from Yalta. My friend was outraged at the unnecessary concessions made by Roosevelt at this summit meeting and did not hesitate to tell him so. Roosevelt in an attempt to reassure him spoke quite frankly.

"These men were in my hand," he said. "But they must have something to show their people at home. If things do not work out well we can always have another meeting and correct them."

To the end he was supremely confident of his ability to win anyone to his point of view. But, as we know, in this case time ran out on him and he did not have another chance.

Both of these men began their careers by using their influence to help others. As we have seen, when this influence, small at first, was developed into great power over millions of people, its corroding influence did its work and they changed, Mussolini in one way, Roosevelt in another. But the point I make here is that they, and countless others, learned to use psychic energy to persuade, influence and, yes, to dominate by starting in a most altruistic and unselfish manner. I urge you to profit from this example and set personal interests aside when you begin your own experiments.

TECHNIQUES OF PERSONALITY INFLUENCE

In employing psychic energy to persuade, three different techniques may be used. They are by:

1. Winning conscious acquiescence,
2. Winning acquiescence without the subject being aware of your influence,
3. Domination.

The first technique is the best, easiest and most often used. In order that you may fully understand how it works let me give you two examples and then I will instruct you in what to do.

In 1959 A.A.H. was working as a salesman for the L.L.L. Company. His headquarters were in the Chicago office, and he was assigned to cover Missouri and the lower half of Illinois below Springfield. His company manufactured many different lines of machinery but in the territory he covered, the farm machinery sold best.

A.A.H. worked conscientiously and well but he soon became aware that the farm machinery products of his company were not their best line and he could never achieve an outstanding success working the down state territory. About this time he learned of the value of psychic energy and decided to apply it to the solution of his problem.

At the earliest opportunity he made a trip to the head office of his company. After having prepared himself in the same manner as I will instruct you later, he presented himself to the general sales manager. After a short delay he was shown into the large office of this leading executive. Let me tell you of that meeting in his own words:

> To my surprise I was not frightened or nervous as I entered his office. Looking back I think I can say I felt confident and slightly curious. I noted that the office was quite large with walls panelled in teak and had three windows facing the north. Through these windows could be seen trees and fields stretching into the distance, for the entire office complex of this huge company was set in a hundred-acre park on the outskirts of St. Paul.
>
> Mr. G. St. J., the sales manager, rose, smiled, shook my hand and motioned me to a seat near his desk. At the time I thought to myself that the preparation I had made was really helping me and my confidence increased. I did not realize then and only learned later that most men in high positions are almost always courteous to those who work under them and it is only the ignorant and crude who are inclined to take advantage of the persons in their employ.
>
> So with confidence and complete candor I explained my problem, little realizing that to a man in his position this was presumption on my part. Yet he listened attentively and when I said I wanted to be transferred to another division, he smiled and said,
>
> "This is an unusual request. It is our company policy to assign our sales personnel according to company needs and not the wishes or whims of the salesmen themselves. However, your courageous approach and candid expression of a desire for greater opportunity have impressed me. Would you be interested in working here at headquarters?"
>
> Of course I said I would be most happy. What an opportunity! I was made assistant to the manager of an entirely new line, a line of school supplies. As you know it was only

a year later that my superior was moved to another division and the school line became my baby. And I don't need to tell you how that baby has grown!

Indeed he didn't. Today A.A.H. is a vice-president of the parent company and the managing director of the educational department, now the second largest division with annual sales exceeding $30,000,000. His story may sound very much like hundreds of other success stories in American business and indeed it is. But unlike many successful men, he actually knows how he got on the path to that success. He knows that the odds against the general sales manager giving him an interview on that day were great to begin with. And there were even greater odds against his listening to and accepting the complaint of a junior salesman who wanted a broader opportunity. And lastly, the odds were probably a million to one against his moving an unknown salesman from down-state Illinois directly into the head office and giving him a minor executive position there. He knows full well that it was the influence exerted by psychic energy that carried him through on that day.

The second example shows the ameliorating influence of psychic energy in a vastly different set of circumstances. It happened not too long ago and concerns a young woman whom we will call Alice. That is not her right name but since she is currently living in New York and quite prominent in business there, her true identity must be protected. In the same way the initials A.A.H. are not the exact initials of the man in the previous example but even so I expect some readers may penetrate this disguise.

Alice was twenty-five years old when the event I am about to describe took place. She had worked since she graduated from high school at the age of seventeen. Because she was intelligent, thorough and hard working she soon made herself indispensable to her employer. She had been trained as a secretary and this was her work when she started. But before very long her willingness to accept responsibility and her competent handling of problems not in her normal line of activity led the owner of the small firm to make her office manager. Two years later her company was bought out by a much larger concern and so it happened that at the age of twenty-four she found herself a successful career woman with an income of $15,000 a year, a pleasant apartment on the East Side and a very comfortable life.

In her reading she had encountered references to psychic energy and had experimented with it in a small way. She had some interesting psychic experiences and believed she might be telepathic but had never actually tested herself seriously. It was about this time that she met Ralph, a new salesman for the company. Almost immediately she found him interesting, which was surprising because he was about her own age. Alice, while only twenty-four, had matured so in her years of work that most men under thirty seemed childish to her. But Ralph was different. He too seemed attracted to her and it was not long before they were seeing each other regularly.

Ralph lived with his mother and it soon became clear that she exerted a major influence in his life and all his activities. He was reluctant to take Alice to meet her and when he did Alice found the mother cold and critical. "If she acts like this when I'm present," she thought, "the Lord only knows what she will say about me after I've gone."

On the way home she asked Ralph if his mother objected to her and if so, why. "She doesn't like any girls I see," he said. "Sometimes she cries if I stay out late and once when I went away for a weekend with some fellows, she got sick." So Alice could see she had a problem and would have to reach a decision either to give up her hope of marrying Ralph or find some way to win his mother over to her side. The thought of parting from this young man who had become so precious to her, who was all she had dreamed of in a mate, was difficult to accept, so she decided to attempt the extremely difficult task of painlessly severing the umbilical cord that still held mother and son together or, better still, of so winning over the mother that she would voluntarily step aside. It was at this point that she thought of psychic energy and asked me if I thought it could help her.

I told her I thought it might but it would depend largely on her own efforts. I instructed her, as I will instruct you, and she started to prepare for a meeting. This preparation covered a two week period but when it was completed she was like a fully charged battery. She was ready and I knew she would not fail.

Afterwards she told me what took place. Using a recent raise in salary as an excuse, she gave a small dinner party in celebration and invited Ralph and his mother. The other guests were nearer the mother's age than her own and one of them was a broadcasting personality of great wit and charm. The evening was a great success and Ralph's mother displayed an unsuspected vivacity, keeping them laughing with her penetrating comments on the public figures of the day.

Toward midnight, as they were leaving, Alice asked Ralph and his mother to stay for a few minutes after the others had gone. When they were alone together, seated in comfortable chairs around a coffee table in her living room, Alice said, "Mrs. B, Ralph and I are very fond of each other. We have considered marriage but I have not agreed. Nor will I unless you approve and give your wholehearted consent."

As Alice told me later, it took all the courage she possessed to make that speech, to deliver what amounted to an ultimatum, and having said it she literally held her breath. But to her amazement and great relief Mrs. B smiled warmly and said, "Darling, I love you. I am sure you will be a most perfect wife for Ralph and I feel he is the luckiest man alive to have won the love of a girl like you. Of course I approve!"

When Alice repeated this to me she actually cried. Through her tears of happiness she said, "It was so perfect. And I owe it all to you. I am so grateful."

This occurred three years ago when Alice and Ralph were twenty-five. They married shortly after and today they are not only supremely happy but exceptionally successful. Now let me explain to you the techniques employed so tellingly by Alice and A.A.H.

HOW TO WIN THE WILLING COOPERATION OF OTHERS

Psychiatrists describe as personal magnetism the ability of certain people to win others over to their point of view. All good salesmen and most top executives have it and use it. In fact a great many people employ this "personal magnetism" but almost no one seems to know what it is or how to get it if you don't have it. You know now that they are using psychic energy and that in order to display this "personal magnetism" you must increase and employ your own psychic energy. Here is the technique.

1. It is better to prepare yourself for several days before attempting a direct confrontation with the person you wish to win over. The more difficult the subject, the longer and more thorough the preparation should be. At least three times each day charge yourself with psychic energy as follows:

Select a place where you will not be disturbed. Then sit in an erect position with your feet touching and your hands clasped lightly.

Breathe deeply to the count of eight, then hold the breath for the count of ten, then release it smoothly and regularly to the count of fifteen. As you breathe in visualize a cloud, white, illumined as if with sunlight and very bright, immediately over your head. As you hold your breath, see the cloud hovering over you and then as you breathe out let it descend gently so that it envelops first your head and shoulders and then your entire body.

Repeat this breathing exercise five times at each sitting and in the beginning practice it at three sittings a day. This is a most potent exercise. It is not unlike charging a battery, only it is you that are the battery and you are charging yourself with psychic energy.

Because you are normally in a relatively run down state, as most people are, frequent chargings are necessary at first. But as you grow stronger and more skillful only an occasional booster will be necessary.

2. For this technique to succeed you must come face to face with the person you wish to influence. When you feel you are ready, arrange a meeting. You will know you are properly prepared when you have practiced several days and feel powerful, confident and commanding. When you come into the presence of the person you wish to influence say or do nothing out of the ordinary. But hold strongly in your mind the project on which you want agreement and at the same time reach out mentally and place your arms about the person almost as if you were embracing him. This is not to be done physically but entirely in your mind as a visualization. Then ask aloud for what you want and if you have done everything right you will get agreement. Usually the other person will go well beyond simple agreement and will aid you in many other unexpected ways.

This is the simplest and most effective way to influence another person to help you. So try it first and do not attempt the next method until you have explored it thoroughly. Now I will tell you of a different approach—how you may win a person to your point of view without him (or her) being in any way aware of your interest at all.

HOW TO WIN AGREEMENT AND COLLABORATION WITHOUT THE SUBJECT BEING AWARE THAT YOU DESIRE IT

This technique is more difficult than the foregoing but when performed properly it will work for you in circumstances where the first technique cannot be used. It is more difficult because it depends for its success on your skill in visualization and also on your ability to convince yourself of the reality of what you are doing. Some teachers describe this as the technique of assumption while others call it the "as if" technique. It is one of the oldest of all occult practices and has been known and used by men as far back into history as records tell us. The ancient Egyptians practiced it more than four thousand years before the Christian era and there are Sanskrit references to it that date even earlier.

Today not only individuals but certain organizations, both religious and secular, have been known to practice it to obtain the objectives which they consider worthy and necessary to their welfare. During World War II a man I knew, whose initials were M. G., wanted to come to the United States from Jerusalem where he lived. Transportation from Palestine or from any other place was next to impossible and what was more important, no visas were being given except to government personnel. For personal reasons, this man, an average citizen with no government rank or influence, felt that his presence in New York was necessary. He wrote me asking that I forward dollars for his passage, which

I gladly did, but I held no hope that he would be able to use them.

To my surprise he appeared at my office about two weeks later. When I asked how he had managed, he said

> I found in each department a person who could approve my passage. In the shipping company it was the man who assigned space, all under priority. I spoke to him, told him it was essential I get to New York as soon as possible since I had no government priority. So I excused myself and said I would return at another time. That night I employed the "as if" technique and when I approached him again the following morning he booked me on a ship leaving Haifa five days later. He gave me no explanation but proceeded as if it were the most natural thing in the world for him to do.
>
> That accomplished, my next problem was a passport and a visa to enter the United States. Each seemed equally impossible but by applying the same technique my way was miraculously smoothed and here I am!

To me this was a most remarkable demonstration. I had a vague knowledge of the "as if" technique but did not realize its potency. Naturally, I plied him with questions and it was from this man that I first learned how to win the cooperation of others by this method.

Here is the technique exactly as M. G. told it to me and which I have proved to myself many times since.

1. Find a secluded place where you will not be disturbed by others or by loud noises from without. This could be an inside room or your own bedroom.
2. Seat yourself in a straight backed chair so you can keep your back erect or lie upon a bed or couch. Either way is satisfactory but many people prefer the chair because they have a tendency to fall into a dream state when lying down.
3. Charge yourself with psychic energy as previously described. Some students state they have found it helpful to intone the sound "AUM" as they release the breath and visualize the psychic energy collecting about them.
4. When adequately charged visualize the person whose co-operation you desire. With your eyes closed see him or

her clearly etched in full detail in the forepart of your brain just behind your forehead.

5. When the visualization is clear feel that you *are* that person, that you are actually inside his or her body.

6. As you begin to realize this quickly think: "I will help that man (yourself) who came to me. He needs help and it is proper that I should give it to him. I can help him easily and without difficulty to myself, so I will do so."

7. Then quickly dismiss the visualization and do not dwell on it again. If possible go to sleep.

This is the entire process. It appears simple and it is simple. Once the visualization is clear and uncluttered by extraneous thought, the other steps should fall quickly and easily into place. As you can see, success depends upon your ability to concentrate to the exclusion of the usual distractions. When you have learned this and acquired a fair degree of skill you will find yourself able to perform this exercise and many others. The accumulation of psychic energy prior to attempting the visualization is very important. This is the wave of energy which carries your wishes into the mind and emotions of the other, where they work to your advantage at the proper time.

PERSONALITY DOMINATION

This is the third technique. It is not recommended as a rule but there are some situations which can only be resolved satisfactorily by employing domination. I strongly advise against attempting it at any time when either of the two preceding techniques will work. While it is true that all too many people dominate or try to dominate others, this is to be deplored rather than emulated. But there are certain times when it is justified.

For example, it is quite right for a doctor to dominate a nervous and fearful patient, calming him and restoring his confidence. An unruly child may and should be dominated by a parent or guardian who is acting in the child's best interest. Most animals, domesticated and wild alike, need to be dominated at certain times. A very capable woman I know had an interesting and amusing experience in this connection not too long ago.

She was staying with her husband at the Jasper Lodge in Jasper National Park in British Columbia. After dinner one night the weather became quite cool and she decided to return to her cottage for a coat. They were living in the last cottage in the long line that strung along the lake from the main lodge, a good quarter of a mile walk. On the way she passed a bear obviously foraging among some papers for something to eat. The bears are completely wild but move freely about the park. They are not interested in people except to cadge sweets from them since these are black bears and not carnivorous. However they are wild animals and likely to turn ferocious at any moment so visitors are warned to stay at a distance from them.

As our heroine passed this huge she-bear nosing about, she felt a stirring of sympathy and decided to bring her some pieces of candy on her way back from the cottage. When she got back to the bear there was no one else to be seen. The two, the huge black bear and small determined woman were alone in the dark forest. Instead of throwing the candy to the bear and walking on, she placed one piece at a time on her flattened palm and offered it to this wild animal as one might to a well trained horse or dog. Very gently, the bear took each piece of candy from her hand with her lips, never showing her teeth. When the last piece was gone and the woman started to walk on to the lodge, the bear followed.

The woman increased her pace. So did the bear. She slowed and the bear came almost alongside. Realizing how alone she was and how foolish she had been, this woman, ordinarily very brave, suffered a moment of panic. Then she took herself in hand. She thought, "If I run, the bear will chase. The bear can run much faster than I can and excited by the chase, may strike me down like any other quarry. No, I can't do that. Obviously the bear wants more candy but I have no more. How would I handle this if it were not a bear but my horse?"

With this thought she knew that she must dominate the bear. So taking three deep breaths she turned to face the bear and said, "Now see here. I have no more candy. See?" and she dusted her hands together. "So you go right straight home!" and she pointed to the deepest forest. Whereupon the bear obediently turned and ambled off in the direction into which she had pointed.

This is a perfect example of animal domination. Employing psychic energy and displaying courage and confidence this small woman commanded a bear six times her size and it meekly obeyed. This was no trained circus animal but a wild bear living in its native mountains, a huge black she-bear with enough strength to kill a man with one blow of her paw, about seven hundred pounds of mischief.

Personal domination is exactly the same. You take the reins in your hands, so to speak. You must have complete confidence in your ability to do so and the slightest chink in your armor of self-possession can lead to failure. When you feel you are in control just tell the subject what he or she should do. The doctor may say sternly: "Stop that shaking and relax. You are all right." The parent may say firmly: "Go to bed. It is now ten o'clock and you need your sleep. Go!" These are very simple examples but in both cases the technique is the same. In a restaurant you may dominate a head waiter who is reluctant to give you the table you desire. This is legitimate. But do not try to dominate another in order to gain an economic or social advantage over him. You may succeed but invariably this will strike back at you when least expected.

The foregoing three techniques for exerting influence on others are practiced unwittingly by many people. Usually they get results without quite knowing how they did it. Very few actually know what has here been described. And very few understand that for genuine success one must carefully avoid injuring others. If you think in advance you can usually see how your objective can be reached with complete harmlessness to all concerned.

By all means, use these techniques, but use them properly. They will give you the satisfaction of achievement, a feeling of power, and will enable you to find success in most of your endeavors.

6

How Psychic Energy Is Used in Dowsing to Find Riches in the Earth, Lost Articles, and People

In a report on July 19, 1967, to a meeting in San Bernardino of the Water Engineers of the State of California, Verne L. Cameron included the following statement.

I live in Elsinore, California, and when our water supply (Lake Elsinore) started to dry up about 20 years ago, I experimented in the area and became convinced that there was plenty of good water underground below the lake bed itself. However the State and U.S. Flood-Control Engineers made a flat statement that there was no water under Lake Elsinore and recommended we purchase Colorado River water from the Metropolitan (Los Angeles) Water District.

It was only after we had spent one million dollars buying the miserable Colorado River water and were refused a contract to purchase a greater annual supply, that our Local Park Board finally drilled an 1800 foot test hole and induced the State of California to complete the well. The test was successful and now, two years later, we have three of the largest wells in Southern California, 1000 feet apart in a line across the middle of the dry end of the seven mile square Lake Elsinore. These wells test out at 5100, 5600 and 5700 gallons per minute respectively under sustained pumping, while the lake itself requires only 6000 gallons per minute to maintain its level in the worst drought years.

The water from these wells is warm, often up to 110° F., and only one grain hard per gallon, while the metropolitan water from the Colorado River is 33 grains hard and contains over a ton of salt per acre foot of water.

The foregoing direct quotation is somewhat technical because it was delivered to a group of Water Supply Engineers, but the man who gave the talk and who was responsible for locating the well sites and having them dug is a dowser, not a water engineer. It was his experiments in dowsing in the area that convinced him that good water was there to be found. It was through his persistence that the hard headed citizens of his community finally agreed to the expense of digging a test well. And it was he who selected the well sites in locations where his experiments indicated that a satisfactory water supply was to be obtained.

WHAT DOWSING IS

Now you may ask, "What is a dowser and what does he do?" Dowsing is an ancient art. Records of dowsing are found in documents written 2000 years ago in the Roman Empire before the time of Christ. In those days and probably long before then the art of dowsing or water-witching was used to locate underground water. The dowser would, as a rule, cut a fresh Y-shaped forked branch from a tree or bush, and using this as an indicator, with the short sections of the Y held firmly in each hand and the long end extending out before him, he would walk to and fro over the area where it was hoped water might be found. Whenever the extended tip of the stick dipped, the spot was marked with a stone or stick, then after the field had been traversed several times, the well would be dug at the spot where the greatest number of markers had been dropped.

The fact that this practice has persisted over two or three thousand years indicates it must have succeeded a large percentage of the time. As far as we know, it was then only used to find water and the ability to dowse was usually confined to but one family in an area, the skill being taught by father to son. These people were often regarded with superstition and in less enlightened times were accused of witchcraft and demonology. Yet we know now that the ability they displayed is a very common one. Four out of five of our troops in Vietnam showed they could dowse with varying degrees of skill and it must be presumed that this average probably holds good for everyone. These combat troops were not looking for water but for booby traps, buried mines and concealed enemy caves and tunnels—which leads us away from the original concept of dowsing into a new and much larger area. Let me explain.

BROAD USES OF DOWSING

For centuries apparently the only purpose of dowsing was to find underground water. Now dowsers are successful in locating lost mines, oil deposits and even ancient sewers and aqueducts. Most dowsers don't understand what takes place. It just works. Nearly every one of them has a theory, some reasonable and some pretty fantastic. The most popular is that water running through the ground creates a magnetic field which attracts the divining rod. Of course running water does create a magnetic field and the scientists who accept dowsing lean heavily on this factor. However there are some respected geologists who maintain all dowsing is nonsense, but they are in the minority and the vast number of successful findings far outweigh their opinions.

The increasing success of dowsers seeking mineral deposits eventually weakened the magnetic field theory and when certain dowsers started locating underground oil and water and minerals from maps it collapsed entirely. Obviously some other factor must be involved and the materialistically minded scientists are completely confused. But as you can see, the real energy employed is becoming evident. It cannot be magnetism or any other measurable physical energy because it works at a distance and responds to thought. The dowsers who work from maps have often achieved remarkable success while 1000 miles distant from the field of exploration. And the man who finds water one day may locate oil the next without any change in technique.

THE SECRET OF DOWSING

The medium used is psychic energy. The dowser who is naturally endowed with psychic energy, or who has consciously accumulated the necessary supply, first turns his thought to the object sought. This directs his psychic energy to the aura of the water or oil or gold. All of these elements have a magnetic radiation which identifies them. Once contact is made the location of water or mineral is then represented to the dowser in the physical manner which he prescribes. This may be the bobbing of a forked stick or the swinging of a pendulum. Successful dowsers all know they employ energy. They may not understand the type of energy they use but they are aware that when they feel strong and "light" they are more accurate than on days when they feel heavy and sluggish. When they finish an arduous session they usually feel depleted and want to rest. One famous dowser said to me that he worked best in places where the air was fresh and sweet and where he could take good deep breaths.

There is an American Society of Dowsers and their headquarters is in Danville, Vermont. They do not espouse any theory of dowsing, realizing that their members come from widely varying backgrounds and have different convictions. But they seek to win wider recognition and acceptance for this art and will gladly give information to anyone who requests it of them. Believing that this manifestation of psychic energy is relatively easy for most people to understand and an avenue many can travel to an ultimate control of this energy, I propose to give you here a brief instruction on how you can become a dowser.

CASE HISTORY OF DOWSING FOR A WELL

Some of you have probably seen a dowsing demonstration, but since most have not I will first describe one to you. We will select a very ordinary search for underground water. A man has purchased a farm and has decided that he needs a water supply for cattle in a distant field. So he has called in a dowser to tell him where to dig the well in order to get the best supply with minimum effort. The dowser has arrived. He looks like any other farmer in the area for this indeed is what he is. His talent as a dowser is not called upon too often and his charges are modest, $50 when he finds water, nothing if he does not. So you can see that for him farming is his livelihood and dowsing an avocation.

He and the owner of the farm have a consultation. The dowser asks where he would like to find water and the purpose to which it will be put. Underground water is usually very pure but it sometimes has mineral or sulfur content which makes it unpleasant to the taste. Such water would not satisfy for household use but would be well suited to the needs of cows and horses. So the owner explains his problem—he wishes to find a water supply for his livestock in a certain field and would prefer a self-flowing well if such could be found. This would relieve him of the need for daily pumping.

Instruments used

Now that the owner's requirements are understood the dowser takes a folded metal instrument from his pocket and prepares to start. The instrument appears to be made of shiny metal wire and it opens up to a T shape. The cross of the T is about 18 inches in length and has a 4 inch length extending down at right angles from each tip. The long arm of the T extends out for 30 inches at an angle of 90° from the cross arm. This is the "divining rod" which the dowser uses to find the water. The owner and dowser then get in a small truck and drive a quarter mile over a bumpy road to the lower field where the animals are pastured. Arriving there the dowser holds the rod in place before him and starts a methodical traverse of the entire field.

Method of operation

The rod is held by the handles, the short four-inch lengths, about chest high with the long end of the T in a vertical or almost vertical position before the dowser. He first goes completely around the square of the field right along the fence lines stopping only once or twice when the tip of the rod seemed to move downward. At each place he stopped he asked the owner to put a colored stake in the ground. After the complete circuit of the field he then started to go back and forth across it much in the same manner as one might when mowing. At about the tenth crossing the rod became agitated and seemed to bend forward almost to the horizontal. The dowser marked this spot with another stake and proceeded to move again at right angles to his previous path. As he walked slowly along the metal rod kept moving up and down bending more and more towards the ground. There seemed to be a point of maximum agitation and when the dowser passed this spot the rod gradually assumed the upright position.

The dowser then retraced his steps along this line and when he came to the point where the pull of the rod's tip toward the ground was greatest he put in another stake. He then carefully circled this stake and put in other stakes wherever the downward pull seemed strongest. By careful checking and cross checking a roughly circular pattern soon appeared and the dowser said to the owner, "If you dig here, I think you will find an adequate water supply at a depth of not more than 16 feet." A well digger was later employed and a fine flowing well discovered 13 feet below the surface.

HOW YOU CAN TRY DOWSING

The foregoing is an actual description of a dowsing for water which took place on the Vermont farm of a friend of mine some years back. It is pretty much the same process as it was a thousand years ago except that today's dowser usually carries his own divining rod with him and for convenience he has made or purchased a folding one. It will be best if your initial attempt at dowsing be made in some similar manner out-of-doors. Use a forked branch or stick as described earlier. Carry it in an inverted Y, with the ends of the fork held lightly in your fingers, palms up and thumbs extending outward. Hold your elbows close to your sides with the arms chest high and the hands about in line with your shoulders. All of the muscles from your hands on up into your shoulders should be held as if they were in one piece, tense but not stiff. Then take three long deep breaths, holding each one in for the count of seven and exhaling slowly to the count of ten. This will give you a slight extra charge of energy and you will be ready to start.

Try this in a field or in a park if you live in the city. Think that you want to find water and walk at random at first until a reaction is felt and a movement in the stick is observed. You may notice this as a slight pull against your wrists as the top of the stick tends to move out and down. Walk slowly about and turn your steps in the direction where the downward pull is strongest. The movement of the stick will become more and more pronounced until a point is reached where a very limber rod will be pointing to the ground. Coordinate your progress with the action of the stick and stop when it has reached its lowest point. You will then be standing over a water vein. Mark the spot, then retreat four or five yards from it and approach it again with the stick held before you. Move slowly so that you do not overrun the critical point. Having assured yourself that the initial spot is correct or nearly so, approach it from several different directions employing the same general procedure. This may enable you to find two or three other locations of maximum pull which will give an idea of whether the water below is a flowing vein or stream or merely a still pool.

USES OF VARIOUS DOWSING INSTRUMENTS

It is not necessary to employ the forked stick, as you know, but a steel rod of the strength of an automobile radio antenna or a wire coat hanger may be used. Actually the marines in Vietnam have used converted coat hangers with excellent success. They clipped off the hook and after straightening out the remaining portion into a single rod, they then bent about four or five inches at one end to an angle of 90°. This leaves a handle for a wand of about 30 inches and with one in each hand the experimenter proceeds as with the cut stick. After instruction and a little practice it was found that many of the men in the U.S. Army and Marine Forces in Vietnam could operate these improvised divining rods quite successfully. They were used to locate enemy tunnels and booby traps and have proved a most valuable substitute for the more sensitive electronic equipment which is usually rendered useless by the concussions and seismic shocks during a bombardment.

Dowsing is also possible with a wand or single stick. Usually it will only work when a substantial amount of psychic energy is employed—much more energy than is required with the forked branch or a similar two-pronged instrument. The wand may be of wood, either newly cut or seasoned, or a standard automobile radio aerial may be used, such as can be purchased in almost any auto supply store. Be sure that the wand has some flexibility but not too much. In other words it should not bend when held out horizontally by the smaller end.

Importance of generating psychic energy

When using the wand be sure to grasp it firmly with both hands by the small end and hold it extended horizontally before you. It is important that you tense all the muscles of your hands, arms and shoulders. Try to keep the muscles on one side working against the similar muscles on the opposite side of your body. This is one way to generate and focus psychic energy. Remember this: *When the art of dowsing works it is because psychic energy is employed and the more energy that is brought to bear, the better the results will be.* From this point onward, proceed just as instructed with the forked stick. The results should be the same.

DOWSING REQUIRES A SPECIFIC WANT

Now we come to a most important point. You cannot dowse for nothing at all. You must be searching for something in order for the stick, or wand, or pendulum, or whatever it is you use, to work. And you must want very strongly to find that something, that water, or oil, or mineral. It is this "want," this desire of yours, that sends out the psychic energy in search of the desired object and it is this want that focusses the psychic energy in such a way that it attunes with and then connects with the object of search. Remember this when you experiment—and you should experiment.

Don't approach this with a skeptical "show me" attitude. This will not work. You must really want to locate something, want that something. If you do and focus enough energy into your hands and arms you will succeed. Try it first where you know there is water or whatever you want. When you find it works, then try it in a strange place. Once you get even the smallest reaction, continue to practice and you will be surprised at how quickly you will improve.

Each person is different. Some dowsers prefer a freshly cut

forked stick, some a folding metal device. Some like a wand while others prefer a pendulum. The use of a pendulum is different and requires special instruction which is set out below.

HOW TO USE A PENDULUM

The same energy, psychic energy, is brought into play when a pendulum is used. Some dowsers find it much easier while others have great difficulty in getting consistent results from it. A pendulum can be made in a variety of ways. Essentially it is a thread or cord with a weight at the end. The thread, cord or chain should be from five to ten inches in length, usually six or seven inches is the optimum, and the weight should not be heavy. A metal coin, a circular eraser, a piece of wood or plastic will in most cases be equally satisfactory. Any weight of an ounce or less should suffice.

The pendulum may be held in several different ways but in essence they all add up to the same thing. You are to hold your hand as motionless as possible and at the same time tense your muscles as greatly as you can without permitting the inevitable vibration that comes from overtension. Take the free end of the cord, the very end of it, between your thumb and forefinger, or between your thumb and the first and second fingers, and hold it about a foot out from your body. Your fingers and thumb should be pressed against each other in order to create the tension necessary to draw the psychic energy into play. If you are planning to use the pendulum out of doors, as in a field in search of underground water, stand erect with your arm level about even with your shoulder and your elbow bent. Point your fingers downward and the back of your hand upward. In this position the thumb and fingers and all of the muscles of your hand, wrist and arm should be strongly tensed. When you walk out over the area of search move slowly and carefully. Try to prevent any jiggling or swaying of the pendulum and see that it hangs down still and straight from your fingers. This may require a little practice.

Remember, you must *want* to find water—or whatever it is you search for. When you are nearing it, the pendulum will start to move on its own. Hold your hand as firm as possible and try neither to retard nor accelerate its movement. Let it move by itself. Sometimes it will move in a circular manner, sometimes back and forth, occasionally from side to side. Once observed, the actual dowsing movement is unmistakable and will never afterwards be confused with the casual bobbing or swaying caused by your general body movement. From this point onward, proceed as you did with the forked stick. The method is the same.

Let me say again that if you dowse for oil you must think of oil and want to find oil. Your "want" then so charges the psychic energy you are bringing into play that it will attune only with oil and your divining rod or pendulum will move only when oil is located. This same concentration of energy can be applied to another object or even a person sought. Just *want* to find it and if it is there your wand or stick will point it out.

EXPERIENCES OF A SKILLFUL DOWSER

To illustrate this, let me relate a couple of experiences of a skillful dowser who lives in Portland, Maine. His name is Norman Leighton [*] and he describes them as follows:

> On my first visit to Deer Isle, Maine, the subject of dowsing came up with my host. He wanted to know if I could determine directions by means of dowsing and I told him I didn't know but would be willing to try.
>
> So my host said, "I have a surveyor's compass which I will use to check you. You have never been on the Island before so the landmarks are not familiar and with the fog you can't use the sun, so let's see what you can do."
>
> Using my folding wand, I asked first the direction to the magnetic north, got a reading and relayed it to my host who had placed the compass on the ground some 25 feet away and was standing over it. He said nothing. I then inquired the direction to the true north, got a reading and relayed that. My host looked baffled. He said, "I don't know how you did it but you were right on the nose in both cases."

A second experience with finding a direction follows:

> I was out in a 19 foot dory with a friend some distance beyond Halfway Rock Lighthouse near the entrance to the Portland harbor when a fog came in. We couldn't see 50 feet in

[*] Norman Leighton, "Dowsing in Down East Maine," *The American Dowser*, American Society of Dowers, November 1967, p. 18.

any direction. I happened to have a rod with me and since there was nothing to lose, I inquired the direction to the wharf on the ocean side of Chebeague Island and after getting a reading we headed in that direction. Periodically, I checked as we went along to make sure we had not drifted or unconsciously altered the course. After about four or five miles we finally came out of the fog and there was the wharf straight ahead about half a mile distant.

Before we leave the pendulum I want to include some pertinent suggestions given by Kate Payne,* a most able dowser who lives in Ithaca, New York.

1. To hold your pendulum properly, arch your wrist so that the string clasped between the forefinger and thumb can have a direct drop. It sometimes helps to extend the last three fingers like antennae.

2. Keep your pendulum in your pocket or close to your body for at least an hour before trying to use it. Then try it at first for short periods only. Don't let anyone else handle it. You want it impregnated with your radiations only. If you don't feel well, don't try. Wait until you do.

3. When dowsing on a map (more on this later) you may support your elbow on the table or not, as you prefer.

4. Your body is a magnet. It has a positive and negative side. Do not cross your hands, arms or feet while working in order to avoid neutralizing the current.

5. When beginning, start with a short string and gradually let it slip out a little at a time.

6. Test for your own personal positive swing. In most cases your right side is positive and the left negative. Separate your knees and hold the pendulum about eight inches above them one at a time. Usually the gyration will be clockwise over the right knee (positive) and counterclockwise over the left. There are exceptions and it may be interesting to find if you are one. Between the knees the pendulum will not gyrate but oscillate back and forth.

* Kate Payne, "Pendulum Pointers for Beginners," *The American Dowser*, American Society of Dowers, November 1967, p. 20.

7. You can use the forefinger of the hand not holding the pendulum as a pointer or antenna. Point it at the subject of experiment.

8. You can test the positive and negative as follows: Let the pendulum suspend from your right hand over a neutral area like a wooden table. It should be fairly quiet. Then touch the positive pole of a bar magnet or a horse shoe magnet with the middle finger of your left hand. The pendulum should start to gyrate in a clockwise direction. Lift your finger, replace it on the magnet's negative pole and observe the change to negative or counterclockwise gyrations. Notice the slight time lag as the force passes through your nerve channels from left hand to right. The same results can be obtained with a dry battery cell from an ordinary flashlight.

9. The pendulum will gyrate over healthy tissue and oscillate over bruised or diseased flesh. Thus it is sometimes possible to locate an injury when it is not outwardly apparent.

10. After some practice you will find your pendulum has become a very personal thing which will help you in many ways. Foods can be tested by you for those which will agree and those which will not with the pendulum gyratrating positively over those good and negatively over those not and oscillating back and forth only over foods which don't matter.

These excellent suggestions by Kate Payne are all based upon her own experience. As she points out, the pendulum becomes a very personal instrument if used often and kept close to the person of the user. However, its reports will also be personal in that it will act in one way for you and another for me. So if you use a pendulum get to know its movements and what they mean. It can then become the interpreter for your conscious mind of the amazing information which your psychic energy obtains.

OTHER DOWSING TECHNIQUES

Most dowsers are rugged individualists. They have acquired their skills through much testing of themselves and the instruments they use and as a result are quite confident of their ability. Not very many can give a good explanation of how they find water or oil, but find them they do, with amazing regularity, and indicate their location with even more surprising accuracy. Still fewer have any conception of the forces at work and the sensitive analyses offered by Kate Payne and by Raymond Willey of Schenectady, another fine dowser, are all the more valuable because so rare.

PSYCHIC ENERGY SECRET OF ALL TECHNIQUES

Because most dowsers have attained their competence through persistent effort, they are prone to overlook the fact that nearly every person has this unique ability to some degree. The experiences of the marines in Vietnam and in their training bases in this country have demonstrated this. Even Hanson Baldwin, who wrote an article on the work of the marines in the field of dowsing for the *New York Times* (October 13, 1967), found that he himself could locate hidden tunnels in his first try. Thus I urge you to test yourself. Remember, the secret which it has taken so many experienced dowsers a long time to learn is that you must supply energy, psychic energy, for best results.

Thus far we have been discussing dowsing done in the field, or on location so to speak. Now I wish to describe for you a different technique, remote or map dowsing. Space limitations here will only permit a general outline but to those of you who may be interested in a very thorough explanation and a course of instruction in this method, I recommend the monographs written by Raymond C. Willey, 959 Norwood Avenue, Schenectady, N. Y. 12303. They are not expensive and can be obtained by writing Mr. Willey.

REMOTE DOWSING

Remote dowsing or "searching," as Ray Willey calls it, can be done from the edge of the field or area to be dowsed or it can be done from a map while many miles away from the area. At first this latter seems so impossible as to be ridiculous but the weight of actual evidence proves it can be done and is being done all over the world. Even certain successful dowsers have viewed map dowsing with skepticism until, finally trying it, their own success convinced them.

The most common form of remote dowsing makes use of the pendulum. The pendulum can be used to give simple "yes" and "no" answers to questions. Usually a back and forth, away-from-the-body and towards-it motion means "yes," while a crosswise motion from shoulder to shoulder means "no." The pendulum also will indicate direction. Standing at the edge of a field, a dowser asks a question. It may be a rather complex question such as "In what direction is the nearest available supply of potable water which will run a minimum of 15 gallons a minute?" If the water is there, the pendulum will answer by swinging back and forth in a line which should be marked. A position should then be taken 100 feet or more away from the original point and at right angles to the line of the pendulum swing and the question repeated. The response of the pendulum should give you a second line which should cross the first line at some point—hopefully within the area in which the water is sought. The area at and around the meeting point of these lines should then be tested in the conventional manner and the well dug where indicated.

Map dowsing is done in a similar manner. The dowser, with a large scale map of the area before him, will say, preferably aloud, "I am at spot X on this map. In what direction will I find the nearest potable water?" The pendulum held before him over the map will start to swing and indicate the direction from spot X in which the water lies. After drawing a straight line through spot X along the line of the direction indicated, the procedure is repeated from another location, spot Y, then a third location is selected, and if all three lines converge on a single point, it is quite certain that the desired water supply will be found there.

DOWSING FOR OIL

Up to this point water dowsing has been the main topic with only a few short references to other uses. First let me tell you of the experience of a dowser who checked an area for some friends and reported that no oil would be found there. This was Ralph Rafferty * of Lakeview, Ohio. He writes as follows.

Some friends of mine have been drilling for oil on a farm-

* Ralph Rafferty, "Oil Dowsing," *The American Dowser*, American Society of Dowsers, February 1968, p. 20.

out from a major oil company and they asked my opinion. Another dowser and I made a simultaneous check, he with their electronic equipment and I with my rod. My results were—no oil, but his equipment gave him a high reading at the site. They had already started drilling and with this encouragement from the electronic tester they continued.

At 700 feet they were in salt water. I had not heard of salt water at this depth in Western Ohio before. They set in 200 feet of 9-inch casing and 910 feet of 7-inch casing to shut out the water. The well was drilled to a depth of 1963 feet into the Trempealean formation and when no oil was found, the well was plugged and abandoned.

They spent four months and a lot of money which might have been saved. In my opinion, the electronic equipment was picking up a reading from the salt water, which was certainly an unexpected hazard as it is not considered a possibility in this area.

Electronic gear vs. dowsing

Here is a conflict between the evidence of electronic gear and psychic energy. The prospectors were drilling because the modern scientific oil locating equipment had indicated that oil was to be found at that location. Now it is quite true that many dry wells have been dug in areas where oil was reported but the significant factor here is that the dowser, using only his natural equipment, made a positive statement that no oil would be found and advised his friends not to continue drilling.

Dowsing for oil same as for water

Oil is located by a dowser in the same manner as water. He simply thinks of oil and asks where oil may be found in the immediate area. Usually the preliminary survey is made on a map with the question asked "Can oil be found in practical commercial amounts at any location on this map?" If the pendulum indicates "yes," then a specific location on the map is selected and the question asked is "In what direction from this location does this oil supply lie?" Then a second line is found to provide triangulation and possibly a third and fourth to provide corroboration.

How to determine depth under surface

At this point the search should proceed to the oil field itself where it may be continued on location by pendulum or rod. The rod and pendulum will record quite accurately the spot under which the oil may be found but it will not indicate its depth from the surface. However, specific requests may be made, such as "Locate the spot under which oil may be found at not more than 500 feet,"—or a thousand feet—or whatever depth seems feasible. In places where the substance sought may be thought to exist close to the surface, as in the case of water, you should stand immediately over the spot where you expect to drill and say "I am going to step out a distance from this spot. When I have gone a distance equivalent to the depth of the water give an indication." Then move out slowly holding your rod or pendulum before you. At a certain point the rod or pendulum will move and become agitated and the distance of this point from the starting place should indicate the depth of the flow.

HOW TO FIND LOST ARTICLES AND PEOPLE

Skilled dowsers have learned much about underground water flow, about oil pools, about mineral deposits and they have even discovered how their dowsing abilities can be used to find lost articles and, upon occasion, lost people. A dowser in Dover-Foxcraft, Maine, located under the ice of the frozen river the bodies of two teen age boys who had been missing for several days. No one had any idea what had become of them but this dowser thought the river presented a possibility and searched there. The police broke into the ice at the first position indicated and found the body of one drowned boy wedged in a rock immediately beneath the opening. The other body was not immediately discovered and the dowser made a second test. He got a fix on a location considerably downstream from the first and the body was found there. It had apparently been carried along by the river flow between the time of the first and second fixes.

DOWSING CAN FIND ANYTHING IF IT IS TO BE FOUND

It appears that the dowsing technique will find anything for you if it is to be found. You need but know definitely what you want to find, visualize it clearly, and want it badly. From that point onward it is just a question of how quickly you can learn to concentrate the psychic energy required. Some people have immediate success. One ten-year old boy I know, the son of a neighbor, was able to get excellent reactions on his first try after being shown what to do. He then went home and confounded his parents by finding coins which his father hid about the house. This was a great game which intrigued everyone and it lasted until his father ran out of coins.

CONFIDENCE THE KEY TO SUCCESSFUL DOWSING

While nearly everyone has the innate capacity to dowse, most people learn the art slowly. It is largely a question of confidence. People look upon this new and strange practice with suspicion. Their early efforts are as a rule diffident and uncertain and of course produce no tangible results. If you are interested, and you should be, you can learn more quickly if you start with an experienced dowser as a guide. Have him demonstrate a "find" and then, knowing where the object is located, try to repeat the performance yourself. His success should give you confidence and his example a visible technique to imitate. However it is true that many fine dowsers have never seen another dowser work and have acquired all their knowledge and skill via the trial and error method.

How dowsing figures in space exploration and war effort

The *London Times* of December 11, 1967, carried a story of an R.A.E. Major who is a competent dowser. The writer, partially impressed and more than a little puzzled, had taken refuge in the sort of tongue-in-cheek writing that many newspaper men use when they are confronted with something they don't quite understand. Here is the article:

DOWSER AMONG SPACE MEN

The most complex situations have always demanded the man with two bits of string, a couple of sticks and a "thing-ummyjig."

The Royal Aircraft Establishment's satellite tracking station at Lasham, Hampshire, gratefully uses the sparetime skills of Major Harold Spary, age 62.

Major Spary, who works in his retirement as the station storeman, is a dowser—one of those impressive people whose talents include mapping underground rivers. His specialty is locating pipes.

Whenever the R.A.E. want to carry on excavation work, Major Spary is the man they call for first.

While around his spartan block house on the station's weather-beaten landscape, trained technicians and a jungle of electronics probe the heavens to plot orbiting satellites, Major Spary with a couple of makeshift rods is out looking for pipes.

Slowly he moves forward, his antennae delicately balanced quivering and swinging before him. "Don't dig there or you'll hit a cable," he advises. The spot is marked and off he goes again. He has helped to plot the tracks of cables and water mains and is said never to have been wrong. If this is so he could well have saved the R.A.E. many hundred pounds.

The Royal Engineers used him during the war in North Africa when they were laying a pipe line from Benghazi to Derna. They used him after the war when they were running new cables to gun emplacements on the South Coast. When asked if he could have detected mines he said "Mines have a habit of detecting you first."

"Anyone can do it," he says, "as long as they have confidence. But don't ask me how. It must be something to do with pressures inside the body."

"Yes, I don't see any reason why I shouldn't be able to find a body or anything else underground. I amuse children by finding pennies under mats." He has a divining fork, too, made of whalebone, which he uses to detect underground water which was extremely useful in the North African desert, but difficult to demonstrate here because you cannot go about digging up airfields to prove you are right.

A widower, he lives at Ropley, Hampshire, with his daughter who dowses and claims to be able to discover the sex of unhatched chickens. He joined the army at 14 and stayed in it 40 years. He fought under Orde Wingate and has served in most parts of the world.

One of these days he will probably start detecting satellites, which will mean an awful lot of electronic equipment going cheap at Lasham.

This short article on Major Spary is but one of hundreds on dowsers and dowsing that now appear each year in various publications. More and more public attention is being focused on this manifestation of psychic energy which so many people demonstrate. This is a technique which can be easily acquired, a technique which will give you a "feel" for psychic energy and the confidence to attempt more sophisticated experiments. Why not try it?

Here are things you can do and some hints as to how to go about them.

HOW TO FIND A PERSON WHO HAS DISAPPEARED AND IS NOW MISSING

1. Use a pendulum as described previously.
2. Hold it firmly in the forefinger and thumb of the right hand and tense your muscles slightly.
3. Rest your right elbow on a desk or table that has been cleared of all other objects and allow the pendulum to hang before you.
4. Then ask aloud, "Is _____ (the name of the missing person) alive?" A motion of the pendulum forward and backward which is to say away from you and toward you indicates "Yes." A sidewise motion from shoulder to shoulder indicates "No."
5. Then stand up and say aloud, "Is he (or is his body if he has been indicated dead) in the direction I am facing?" Hold the pendulum as before firmly in the thumb and forefinger of your right hand. Bend your right elbow so that the pendulum will hang before you at about the level of your heart.
6. If the response is "No" turn slightly, maybe about one eighth of a full circle and repeat the question.
7. When the answer is "Yes" stay facing that way and seek to find the distance.
8. Start by asking, "Is he less than 100 miles from here?"

If the answer is "No" change the question to 200 miles and so on until you get a "yes" reaction.

9. If you get a "Yes" answer to the 100 mile question then ask "Is he less than 50 miles?" Continue to narrow down the bracket until you find the exact distance.

10. You will then know the direction and the distance. Go to that place and proceed with the pendulum as before for direction, then distance. Only now you ask in feet, not miles.

If you assume that the person you seek has merely gone to some distant point you can use a map. Once direction and distance have been determined a large scale map can be used. For example if you are in New York and you have determined the person you seek is in Miami, obtain a street map of Miami and Miami Beach and proceed as follows:

1. Say "I am standing on the 79th Street Causeway where it enters Miami Beach and I am facing due west along the causeway. Is he in this direction?"

2. By shifting very gradually and asking the same question you can determine his direction from that key spot you have selected. Then you can proceed to determine the distance and when this is known hold the pendulum over the map and say, "When I hold this pendulum over the exact spot where he is located, signify by the positive circular movement."

3. It is best to do this part of the experiment at night about 2 or 3 A.M. in order to make sure the person you seek is in his home. The pendulum will locate the person wherever he may be at the moment the question is asked and he could be at work or at dinner or visiting, etc.

Much the same procedure should be followed when seeking a lost article. In this case the distance is not apt to be very great. So start with 50 feet, not 50 miles. Be sure to see the article quite clearly in your mind's eye when you question for its location.

Don't have a confused or changing image or you will have a confused result.

One more suggestion. Always take three deep breaths before starting an experiment and if it should continue over long, repeat this breathing technique to "recharge your batteries," so to speak.

7

How Psychic Energy Enables You to See Yourself and Others As Having Appeared in Past Lives

One of the remarkable gifts of psychic energy, a talent to which almost any person may aspire, is the ability to see different visages of past lives superimposed on the face of another, or on one's own in a mirror. This introduces the idea of reincarnation, the belief that we live again and again. The concept is not readily accepted by the average western mind yet more than half of all the people in the world take it for granted. Just as they know they were born, and that some day they will die, they believe with equal certitude that they have lived many lives before the present, and will experience many new and different incarnations in the future.

A REINCARNATIVE EXPERIENCE

When we are small and as we grow up we accept without question the beliefs of our elders and contemporaries. In the Christian world, which means western civilization in general, everyone is taught that we live but one life, the present. When I first had reincarnation explained to me I could not accept it and it was not until I had personal experiences of the type I will now describe that I changed my mind. The strange thing about a belief deeply ingrained in early childhood is that it can but seldom be altered by reasonable argument. As a rule, an actual experience is necessary before conviction is possible.

This was true in my case. I was told to experiment with a mirror in a manner I will explain in detail later in this chapter. I proceeded as instructed and after having settled myself comfortably I gazed intently at my reflection in the mirror. After about three minutes the image started to ripple and distort much as if I were looking into a pool of water which had suddenly been stirred.

"This is eye fatigue," I said to myself and blinked two or three times to clear my vision. To my surprise the distortion commenced again almost immediately and as I watched I saw the outlines of my face change. From the visage of a young man of thirty three with heavy dark brown hair the face in the mirror became that of a much older man. The hair receded so that the fore part of the head was bald and a grayish wiry brush remained at the back and sides. The face broadened, the jaws filled out and the skin became paler as a gray scruffy beard appeared over the jaws and chin.

I was horrified. "Can this be me?" I thought, "If so, when? Who was I? Was I ever such an ugly old man?" It was only some years later, as I pursued my studies, that I found out more about that person who had lived so many, many years ago. I came to realize then that, ugly as he seemed to me at the time, he had nevertheless exerted a profound and beneficent influence upon my present life and abilities.

AN EVIDENTIAL APPROACH TO REINCARNATION

There is ample evidence for reincarnation but most western minds reject the evidence itself. Dr. Ian Stevenson, an M.D. and the head of the Department of Neurology and Psychiatry of the University of Virginia's School of Medicine, recently published a book modestly titled *Twenty Cases Suggestive of Reincarnation.**

* Dr. Ian Stevenson, *Twenty Cases Suggestive of Reincarnation*, New York, American Society for Psychical Research, 1966.

These twenty case histories are but a representative handful of hundreds of such which he explored in the widely separated areas of India, Ceylon, Brazil, Alaska and Lebanon as well as here in the United States. Each "history" in the book gives in a most detached and scientific manner the evidence painstakingly gathered by Dr. Stevenson in personal interviews with the persons concerned, their families, other witnesses and in some cases from court records. This evidence is most impressive and will convince any open-minded person. Yet many reject it, usually without reading it thoroughly. So I realize full well that a statement to the effect that he has lived more than once is usually rejected without further consideration by the average westerner. Only a personal experience will convince him otherwise. It is for this reason I am here including a short paragraph below on a little known but quite important human ability which can be developed by employing psychic energy, the ability to actually see your appearance and that of others in certain past lives.

A TECHNIQUE FOR SEEING INTO PAST LIVES

Here is the technique. *First,* calm yourself. If you are in any way physically upset or disturbed emotionally you will get no results. It is almost like trying to see the bottom of a lake when the surface has been disturbed by winds or when the water itself is muddy. So put off your attempt until you are thoroughly relaxed and quite calm.

Second, charge yourself with extra psychic energy. The simplest method is one already suggested, namely to take five deep breaths, hold each one for the count of ten and then exhale slowly over the count of fifteen, all equally cadenced. Relaxed and charged with energy you are now ready.

Third, if you plan to examine yourself be sure you are alone and will not be disturbed. Set a large mirror, at least 10 x 12 inches or larger on a table or desk before you as you seat yourself in a straight backed chair. Extinguish all light in the room except a single candle which should be placed to the left of the mirror and in your line of vision.

Fourth, compose yourself and look steadily at yourself in the mirror. Say to yourself "I would like to see what I looked like in one of my previous lives." Then while remaining otherwise relaxed, strain your eyes slightly as you look directly into the eyes in the mirror. If you find you have an inclination to squint slightly as you do this, it is all right. Just try to establish and maintain a tension in your eyes themselves. You will, as a rule, notice first a tendency for the mirror to cloud over and obscure your image. This will come in flashes and change quite rapidly. Next there may appear a shimmering in the mirror almost like looking into a rippled pool. This is an indication of the activity of your psychic energy on the subtle vibrations of the chemical crystals of the air itself. Then sometimes gradually and sometimes quite rapidly your image will change. Often the reconstruction will begin not in an alteration of the facial lines but in some details of headdress or clothing. The very character of the face will change quite imperceptibly and in the most unexpected features. Rarely will your facial image hold to its present type. Do not prolong the experiment as it puts a strain on the eyes. *Ten minutes at the most should be ample.*

True nature of this experiment

This is not psychic sight or what is usually called clairvoyance, but actual physical sight using the optic nerve. The psychic energy acting under your request so stimulates the optic centers that by slight additional effort, like trying to pierce a fog or look into the distance, a different dimension is brought into range of your normal eyesight. This experience can be most convincing. Try it.

Let me add that this is not autosuggestion. If you are honest with yourself, you will know that you had no previous knowledge of the appearance perceived. It may be pleasant or it may be nondescript. On the other hand it may be noble and inspiring or it might be terrifying. In all events you will see something strange and far different from anything you may expect.

How to experiment with another person

After you have tested this with yourself try it with another person. Be sure you two are alone. If others are present they can influence the action of the psychic energy and either produce a distorted result or nullify the action entirely. Reduce the lighting to a single shaded lamp or a candle placed in your line of vision slightly to your left as you face the person you are about to study. Sit about four or five feet apart and face each other directly. When you and your subject are thoroughly composed take the deep breaths as indicated and then look steadily into the eyes of your subject.

Say aloud, or quietly to yourself, "I would like to see the appearance of this person (using the name is best) in a past life." Then concentrate your gaze and continue to look directly into the eyes of your subject, not elsewhere. As you strain your eyes and even squint a little you will notice the shimmer which usually precedes the change. Do not continue this concentration for more than ten or at the most fifteen minutes. Then stop and do not repeat the attempt with either the same person or another until at least an hour has passed.

This is a very ancient practice. It was employed by certain Egyptian priests as far back as 2500 B.C. The priests who served the Pharaoh were often called in to examine witnesses in state and judicial matters. Then it was not the appearance of a past life that was sought but the inner appearance of the man testifying. When the testimony was over the priest would privately tell the Pharaoh or the presiding justice whether the witness had spoken truly or not for this also is discernible to the concentrated gaze augmented by psychic energy. The subtle changes which could be observed by the highly trained priests also provided a barometer of illness and health as well as disturbances of the spirit. These priests were sincere, spiritual men whose abilities were enhanced by their pure and dedicated lives. Similarly today while it is true that almost everyone can perform this experiment and achieve recognizable success, it is the pure in heart, the well-intentioned persons of good will, who find it possible to go on to much more dramatic demonstrations.

Author's personal experiences

To make this clearer I will describe a few actual experiences of my own.

I was sitting at lunch in a crowded restaurant, not the best possible environment, directly facing this man. He was gray-haired with a ruddy complexion like many English and Irish types. He was telling me that he had recently finished translating the Aphorisms of Patanjali, his own translation, and was now writing a book about this great mystic and incorporating in it quotations from his philosophy. As he talked the noise in the room faded into the background and his face started to change. From a ruddy faced Britisher he became a thin-faced ascetic with cocoa brown skin and very little hair. His blue eyes changed to dark brown and shone with an inner fire. It was gone in a moment but in that small fraction of time I saw and realized the reason for his present dedication to Patanjali.

I interrupted him and told him what I had seen. To my amazement his face changed once again. It broadened, it became younger and much more powerful. The smile bespoke the confidence of one who had never known failure and he appeared to be laughing almost gleefully. There it was, a complete metamorphosis. Within seconds it changed, and the mild, 60 year old scholar was again before me while the restaurant chatter about us became just as deafening as before.

This experience was unsought and entirely unexpected. Occasionally such episodes will occur after you have adjusted yourself to this new ability. But in the beginning it will be necessary to proceed as I have described.

It happens once in a while that instead of a personality from a past life you will pick up a slightly different manifestation. Here is an example.

A young woman of about 28 years of age, the mother of three small children, asked me to read her. It was not possible to achieve privacy since we were in a room with about forty others but we finally found a not too crowded corner. I asked her to continue to talk about anything that occurred to her and meanwhile I tried to see beyond the physical appearance before me.

Quite suddenly she was a child, a round-faced serious dark-eyed little girl of about six. This held for some twenty seconds, much longer than usual. Then without my fully realizing it the woman started talking about a philosophical subject and just as quickly her appearance changed. Her hair was still dark but differently arranged and her age appeared to be about 50. Her face became thinner and graver and much more beautiful yet retained some of her original appearance. Having seen this I terminated the sitting.

After a short reflection I realized that what I had seen were not appearances from past lives but two periods in her present life, one as a small child, an appearance from the past, and the other as a mature woman some twenty years in the future.

REINCARNATION AS AN ESTABLISHED ANCIENT FACT

It might be well at this point to tell a little more about reincarnation. At the time of Christ and prior to then all thinking people, all educated people and many others who had no education at all accepted without question and as a fact that we all live again and again in different bodies. There are still many references to reincarnation in both the Old and New Testaments even though the fifth ecumenical council at Constantinople ordered all such references culled from the text and pronounced fourteen soul-searing anathemas on anyone who thereafter dared to teach or to hold to that belief. Certain conversations between Jesus and His disciples indicate their curiosity as to who He might have been in a previous life. When there was some speculation as to whether He might have been the Prophet Elias, He soon set them right (Matthew, Chapter 16:14, Chapter 17:10-13) by indicating that Elias had been reborn as John the Baptist. And there are several other such instances.

REINCARNATION IN THE MODERN VIEW

In modern times the Roman church has taken a broader view. Cardinal Mercier stated not long ago that a belief in reincarnation is permissible, prominent bishops in the Church of England openly espouse it, and hard-headed American businessmen like Henry Ford and Thomas Edison expressed their conviction that they have lived before and will live again. Many people today have experienced a comfortable familiarity when visiting a strange place for the first time. You yourself may have had such an experience. Could this not be a memory?

THE CASE OF JOEY VERWEY

Magazines, books and Sunday supplements have in the last few years carried many stories about children who recall previous identities and name places and relations with vivid detail. One such case recently reported concerns a pretty dark-haired teen-age miss named Joey Verwey who lives in South Africa. She is fond of drawing, but when she puts pencil to paper the sketches produced show scenes from many years ago. These are reproduced with such remarkable detail and supported by such complete verbal descriptions that historians have been forced to the conclusion they accurately represent actual scenes. This conclusion was forced upon them when certain details, previously unknown, were found upon investigation to be true reproductions.

Joey says she lived in South Africa in the life immediately preceding the present and actually singled out an 80 year old woman to whom, she said, she had given birth in that life. Her parents in their concern for her sanity took her to a well known doctor, Arthur Bleksley, M.D. of the University of Witwatersrand, South Africa. He arranged for a meeting between Joey and her 80 year old former daughter and was amazed to hear her describe the circumstances of birth, the death of her husband, the father, shortly thereafter, the move from Ireland where she originally lived to London where she married again, and to have all this corroborated by the equally astounded old woman.

Joey said that after moving to South Africa, in that previous life she had known the then President Oom Paul Kruger and had visited his house in Pretoria. Paul Kruger died in 1904 and his home was subsequently turned into a museum. Doctor Bleksley decided to test her on this and after ascertaining that little Joey had never been to Pretoria, he took her there. As they approached the house and before entering Joey described certain rooms and the furniture they had contained years ago. Some of the furniture was still in place and the custodian confirmed the description she gave of other articles.

Joey remembers other lives but thus far no way has been found to check them out as thoroughly as her life in the Transvaal. She can recall an amazing amount of detail and on occasion she has been challenged by historians and experts on the period in question. In every case, additional research has proved her observations correct and the initial opinion of the expert in error.

REINCARNATIVE EXPERIENCES OF A MONK

Another such case recently in the public press concerns a Buddhist monk, Phra Rajsuthajarn, living in Thailand. He claims to have a complete recollection of his previous existence. He was a farmer named Leng who lived not far from where he was born. Leng had three daughters who are still alive. They told how the present monk had said his name was Leng as soon as he could talk. He knew Leng's daughters and called them by name as well as many other relatives. He described in detail the circumstances of Leng's death and cremation, how the body was first laid out on a mat and then after the incineration the bones were brought back to the house where he had lived.

The venerable Phra Rajsuthajarn also brought into this life another interesting memory. Leng had travelled, and while in Laotia had learned to speak the language. No one in the community of Phra Rajsuthajarn had any knowledge of this language, yet one day when some Laotians visited his monastery, he found unexpectedly that he was able to understand and converse with them.

At the age of 16 Leng had entered a Buddhist monastery where he learned the Cambodian script in order to read certain sacred manuscripts. He left the monastery at 25 and became a farmer. When the venerable Phra entered a Buddhist monastery he was taught in Siamese, his native language. However he one day encountered some of the sacred Pali texts and although they were written in Cambodian characters, a language quite different from Siamese, he had no difficulty in reading them.

Leng's first daughter, Mrs. Pah, said she was about 22 when her father died. She was at that time married and had a child of her own. When little Phra, age 4, saw her he recognized her immediately and said "I am your father" and called her by a baby nickname. Her first reaction was one of annoyance because she felt that as a married woman and a mother she was entitled to more respect from a 4 year old. It was only after he had similarly addressed Leng's second daughter Mrs. Poh that the sisters regarded him seriously and questioned him further. The third daughter, a Mrs. Pi, gave similar testimony and added that as a child Phra Rajsuthajarn had described many incidents in the life of Leng which she knew had occurred.

This case is well known in Thailand and has been investigated by several learned authorities there. Films of the family have been made and shown on television and the Leng-Phra history has been given wide publicity in the press and periodicals. In that country this is regarded as good evidence of what everyone knows and believes but seldom has demonstrated so conclusively.

PSYCHIATRISTS' USE OF REINCARNATION

In the last ten years some psychiatrists have been using hypnotism to regress patients back to childhood in order to discover if a traumatic experience may have occurred then which is causing emotional imbalance and distress today. Occasionally the doctor in charge, not finding anything of significance in the present life, will regress the patient to a previous life. Much interesting evidence is being obtained in this way, evidence not only of reincarnation but also of the way physical and emotional damage in one life will frequently affect a later incarnation.

OTHER TYPES OF EXPERIENCES

Certain more imaginative researchers have asked their subjects to describe their existence between incarnations and the reports obtained agree almost entirely with one another. Apparently for most people this is a time when they evaluate the life just left and plan how they may best employ the life to come in order to advance to that state of being where it will no longer be necessary to return to earth in a physical body. While the existence on the spiritual plane is much more pleasant, nearly everyone there is so eager to make progress he willingly leaves it when the opportunity to occupy a new body presents itself.

Many well known people hold the conviction that they have lived before in another body, and usually this belief stems from some sort of personal experience. Samuel Clemens, who wrote under the name of Mark Twain, did not have the slightest doubt he had lived many different lives in the past. All his life he had certain dream experiences which had the impact of reality. He kept written records of them intending apparently to weave them into a treatise on reincarnation or possibly even a novel. These notes were found after his death and posthumously published under the title "The Mysterious Stranger."

The experiences all centered about a single character, a young girl of about fifteen whom he met and loved in different lands at different times. She had many names and her appearance differed from one personality to another but for him her identity did not change. These experiences started when he was in his twenties and continued for more than forty years, recurring about once every two years. They were impressive in their emotional and sensible impact and in their wealth of detail. He describes one experience as follows:

> It was sudden. There I was, crossing a wooden bridge that had a wooden rail and was untidy with scattered wisps of hay, and there she was, five steps in front of me. This was the exit of the village which lay immediately behind us. Its last house was the blacksmithshop and the peaceful clinking of the hammers—a sound which nearly always seems remote and is always touched with a spirit of loneliness and a feeling of soft regret for something, you don't know what—was wafted to my ears over my shoulder; in front of us was the winding country road with woods on one side and on the other a rail fence with blackberry vines and hazel bushes crowding its angles; on an upper rail a blue bird and scampering toward him along the same rail a fox-squirrel with his tail bent high like a shepherd's crook; beyond the fence a rich field of grain and far away a farmer in shirtsleeves and straw hat wading knee-deep through it; no other representatives of life, and no noise at all, everywhere a Sabbath stillness.
>
> I remember it all—and the girl, too, and just how she walked, and how she was dressed. In the first moment I was five steps behind her; in the next one I was at her side. I put my arm around her waist and drew her close to me, for I loved her. She showed no surprise, no distress, no displeasure, but put an arm around my waist, and turned her face to mine with a happy welcome in it, and when I bent down to kiss her she received the kiss as if she was expecting it, and as if it was

quite natural for me to offer it and her to take it and have
pleasure in it.

We strolled along across the bridge and down the road
chatting like the oldest friends. She called me George and
that seemed natural and right though it is not my name; and
I called her Alice and she did not correct me. Everything that
happened seemed just natural and to be expected. Once I
said, "What a dear little hand it is!" and without any words
she laid it gracefully in mine for me to examine it. I did it re-
marking on its littleness, its delicate beauty and its satin skin,
then kissed it; she put it to her lips without saying anything
and kissed it in the same place.

Mark Twain tells many such experiences, all of them vivid,
colorful, intimate and very, very real. In each he identifies the
same young girl though her appearance changes. At one time she
is the country lass described in the foregoing, at another a composed beauty in ancient Athens and in still another she is an exotic
dancer in Hawaii. He was convinced these episodes were scenes
recalled from previous lives and through this intensely personal
evidence he came to believe in reincarnation.

Another well known writer, Joan Grant, also was led to accept
the idea of reincarnation through her own personal experiences.
From her earliest childhood she could remember snatches of other
existences. When young she took this for granted and assumed
everyone else recalled similar experiences but were merely reticent
about them. It was only as she approached the age of thirty, had
married and borne a daughter that she succeeded in bringing
through into her conscious recollection long sequences from one
life or another. It was about this time that she learned to distinguish between fact and fancy, between a self-created thoughtform and a scene which had its own objective reality. For example if in her vision she saw two people approaching, one
cloaked in red and the other in green, and she could wilfully
change the colors, then she knew it to be only a thoughtform. But
if the scene could not in any way be altered no matter how intently
she tried to change it, it was then accepted as a factual recollection.

With her these "recollections," as she calls them, seemed exactly like memories, particularly vivid memories, of events which

may have happened last week or at the most distant maybe a month back. All of the details including emotion and sensation were so vivid that the experience would seem like the factual present. Miss Grant (now Mrs. Denys Kelsey) explains that in order to recall lengthy sequences of other lives she had to learn how to shift the level of her attention from the present personality to the earlier one and still retain enough waking consciousness to be able to report a running commentary, not only of the experience but also of the earlier personality's thoughts, emotions and sensations. Her reports on the experiences of one life were so complete and so vivid that she compiled them into chronological order and had them published. She called the story "The Winged Pharaoh" and it was originally regarded as a remarkably researched work of fiction. But when archaeologists and Egyptologists discovered in this account certain facts and explanations about the life in Egypt 4000 years ago which had not hitherto been known, and when they had gone to the available records and verified that these were logical and most reasonable, a wave of interest was aroused. The book came to be looked upon by Egyptologists as an invaluable source of information on the First Dynasty period in Egyptian history, and by most open-minded readers as a true account of a previous life.

It was in this manner that Joan Grant convinced not only herself but many others that all of us live many lives and occupy many different bodies in the course of our existence. You too can convince yourself of this strange fact, convince yourself in your own way, and in the doing learn a great deal about your unknown abilities and hidden talents.

A WORD ABOUT MORE SOPHISTICATED EXPERIMENTS

So now let us go back to the beginning of this chapter. Remember the experiment with the mirror? Try it and see what happens. When you succeed you will gain confidence and the courage to attempt some of the more sophisticated experiments which will be explained in succeeding chapters.

8

The Role Psychic Energy Plays in the Apports Presented in Spiritualistic and Similar Paranormal Manifestations

Let me say right at the beginning of this chapter that a great deal of the activity which takes place in Spiritualist churches and at spiritualistic seances is perfectly honest and genuine. But, unfortunately, not all. The best spiritualists themselves will tell you this and deplore the fact. The relatively intangible character of the results achieved in the average spiritual reading or sitting presents a temptation to those who use it as a means of livelihood. In a very normal desire to give the sitter "something for his money" a less talented medium sometimes will make shrewd guesses and support them with a little showmanship. Their exposure has unfortunately cast a shadow over all spiritualist practice and has increased the skepticism of the vast majority.

This is unfair. It is possible to communicate with certain individuals who dwell beyond the curtain of death and for them to communicate with us. The connecting link in almost every case is forged of psychic energy. I say "almost" because we are here exploring unknown territory and must guard against a very normal human tendency to put everything that looks alike into the same package. There are many ways in which this intercommunication takes place. Even a most detailed accounting would cover but a fraction of those which have been reported and there are presumably a great many others. The most common however are via automatic writing, the planchette, the voice of a medium, direct voice, apports, symbolic appearances and actual appearances. These we will consider here because for the most part they represent objective experiences which presumably can be observed by disinterested persons apart from the medium and the sitter. The vivid dreams, certain feelings or impressions not experienced by others and similar purely subjective experiences will be discussed in another chapter. Now, let us look at automatic writing.

AUTOMATIC WRITING

There are literally thousands of recorded cases of automatic writing, some of them quite famous. One of the best known and most remarkable is the book *OAHSPE*, sometimes called the *OAHSPE Bible*. It was written by Dr. John Ballou Newbrough and copyrighted in 1882.

John Ballou Newbrough was born on a farm near Wooster, Ohio on June 5th, 1828. From his early youth he indicated some ability toward both clairvoyance and clairaudience, which were brought more fully to the surface during his college days as a result of being mesmerized (hypnotized) by a Professor Sutherland. He studied dentistry and practiced in California and Australia before finally settling in New York.

Dr. Newbrough in his middle life developed remarkable mediumistic ability. Under instruction from an unseen guide, who used Newbrough's hands (and his psychic energy) to write out his orders, he practiced certain disciplines for ten years and then set about the writing of *OAHSPE*. In that period of training he gave up eating meat and fish, milk and butter. He rose each day before the sun and bathed twice a day. His weight dropped from two hundred and fifty pounds to one hundred and eighty and remained fixed there; rheumatism which had previously bothered him left him entirely and he was no longer subject to minor ills such as headache, colds and indigestion. He seemed to have taken a new lease on life.

About this time he was instructed to buy a typewriter and learn to type. This he did with difficulty but after two years he had acquired a fair degree of skill and his actual writing began. Each morning for a half hour just before sunrise he sat at his desk while his fingers flew over the keys. This continued for fifty weeks at the end of which time he was told to read what he had written, which he did and states he was amazed at what he found there.

That his writing was "automatic" can hardly be questioned. The book itself is of such a scope that it seems improbable that any one man, or even a committee, could write it in a lifetime. Yet even if we set this impressive document aside, his practice of writing with both hands simultaneously when blindfolded or in darkness, and occasionally of drawing skillfully with one hand while writing with the other seems to give evidence of direction well beyond the normal.

Writing on January 21st, 1883, to the Editor of the "Banner of Light," a Boston publication, he included the following statements:

Some years ago, Oahspe was mechanically written through my hands by some other intelligence than my own. Many Spiritualists are acquainted with automatic movement of the hands, independent of one's own volition.

There are thousands and thousands of persons who have this quality. It can be educated, or rather, the susceptibility to external power can be increased.

The title page of OAHSPE carries the following statement:

A Kosmon Revelation in the words of Jehovih and His Angel Ambassadors. A Sacred History of the Dominions of the Higher and Lower Heavens of the Earth for the past Twenty Four Thousand years from the Submersion of the continent Pan in the Pacific Ocean, commonly called the Deluge, to the Kosmon Era. Also a brief history of the Preceding Forty five Thousand years together with a Synopsis of the Cosmogony of the Universe; the Creation of the

Planets; the Creation of Man; the unseen worlds; the Labor and Glory of Gods and Godesses in the Etherean Heavens; with the New Commandments of Jehovih to Man of the Present Day; with revelations from the Second Resurrection, formed in words in the thirty third year of the Kosmon Era.

As you can see, it offers quite a bit of surprising information in great detail and covers nearly 1000 pages of small type with two columns to a page, almost 1,000,000 words. This is no small task to have accomplished in less than a year.

To me there seems no doubt that Dr. Newbrough wrote automatically and that his hands were guided by an intelligence or intelligences superior to his own. But the energy employed in the writing was his and the energy used to guide his hands was also his own psychic energy accumulated in great quantities throughout his years of preparation. Psychic energy is obedient to mental direction and while the energy was Dr. Newbrough's, the direction came from some other source, a highly intelligent and well-informed source. The identity of this source and its nature can only be surmised from the writing itself. Read it and draw your own conclusions.

INSTRUCTIONS FOR AUTOMATIC WRITING

If you would like to experiment with automatic writing follow these instructions.

1. Always take a bath before any automatic writing session. This is not only to cleanse yourself physically of impurities that may be clinging to you but it is also symbolical of a spiritual cleansing which should take place before exposing yourself to any foreign influence.
2. Sit at a desk or table where you will not be disturbed and compose yourself.
3. When you are completely relaxed physically, calm emotionally, and clear mentally, take three deep breaths letting each one out quite slowly.
4. Then take pen or pencil in your hand, place it on the top line of the blank pad before you, see that your arm is comfortable and relax.

You may get a response the first time but more likely not. So try again and repeat the preparation here outlined each time. If after a serious attempt, on five different occasions, you get no result, set the idea aside temporarily and try it again in a year when you and conditions about you will have changed.

If your hand starts to write, it may turn out serious material or it may write nonsense. If the latter, stop immediately and try again another time, making sure you prepare yourself most carefully. Foolish, childish or confused writing is evidence of a poor connection (so to speak) or contact with a low grade personality. If this occurs, try the next time to raise the level of your consciousness by clearing your mind of low-grade thoughts and impulses. Usually you can establish a satisfactory mood by prayer, or by reading a passage from the Bible or another inspirational work.

When you get a serious response, do not hesitate to ask aloud "Who is this?" You will, as a rule, get a completely candid answer to this and to any other legitimate question that may occur to you. Once you have learned how to relax your hand and arm and have caught on to the proper "don't care" attitude, interesting results should ensue. Automatic writing is not something new, or strange, or so very different. Many people practice it and there are literally thousands of books, documents and reports written this way that are available for examination.

A book written by a discarnate author

There is another book you may find interesting. It is titled *A Dweller on Two Planets*.* Its writer, Frederick S. Oliver, disclaims any credit for it saying that it was written automatically under the guidance of a discarnate intelligence he identifies as Phylos.

Frederick Oliver was born in Washington, D.C., in 1866, the son of a medical doctor who moved his family shortly thereafter to California. At the age of 17, in 1884, he started writing automatically and found he was producing material far beyond his experience and limited mental capacity. The author of this material eventually identified himself as Phylos, the Esotericist. For

* Frederick S. Oliver, *A Dweller on Two Planets*, Los Angeles, Poseid Publishing Company, 1924. Now published by Borden Publishing Co., Los Angeles.

a year Phylos trained Oliver and showed him how he could increase his psychic energy. His whole being became more refined until he could actually hear Phylos as well as respond manually to his direction. The manuscript was begun in Yreka, California, in the winter of 1883 84 and finished in Santa Barbara in 1886. It remained in manuscript until 1894 when it was copyrighted.

The book is remarkable not only in its scope and breadth of vision but also because it tells of many scientific devices that were unknown in 1886 but since invented, and many others which have not yet been produced but whose development now seems likely. For example, a form of television is described and there is visual and audible electronic communication over a distance of 7000 miles. There are aircraft without wings which move at 1000 miles an hour and maintain altitude by means of magnetism in the form of a gravity nullifier. The United States government at the present time is spending many millions on research into just this form of air travel and it seems likely that a breakthrough is not too far off. X-Ray machines and their uses are described and in 1886 these were unheard of. In a word this book is unusual and a classic example of the highest type of automatic writing.

THE PLANCHETTE

Another form of automatic writing which has in recent years been treated as a parlor game is the use of a numbered and lettered board sometimes called a "Ouija Board." This is a rectangular board about ¼ inch thick and usually two by three feet in area on which are printed the numbers one to nine plus a zero and a place for "Yes" and "No." Also on the board are all the letters of the alphabet arranged as a rule in a sort of semicircle or arc. The surface of the board is quite smooth to facilitate an easy motion by the "planchette." This is a small flat piece of wood about two by three inches in area which sits up on three legs. One end is rather pointed and this end is used to select and come to rest over the various letters and numbers as a message is spelled out.

Methods of operating planchette

The energy employed is psychic energy. Sometimes one person can operate it quite well by placing one or both hands lightly on the "table top" of the planchette as it rests upon the board. However in a vast majority of instances beginners will fare better if two people cooperate, with each placing one hand lightly on the planchette. This increases the supply of psychic energy to a point where the experiment can be performed. Here is one standard technique of operation:

> Place the board on a table and sit comfortably before it. If two people are to participate, it will be simpler and easier if they sit at opposite sides of the table facing each other. Place the hands lightly on the planchette and make no attempt to lean on it, press on it or in any way urge it in one direction or another. Just let the fingers touch it lightly and when it moves, allow your hand and arm to follow the motion without influencing it in any way.

> When you are properly prepared, ask a question aloud—any question. You may get an immediate reaction or you may not. Keep calm and relaxed and wait. As a rule you will get some response after three or four minutes. In such cases the planchette will move, apparently of its own volition. The energy moving it is psychic energy, your psychic energy and that of your companion if you have one. This is not muscular movement. If anything, your muscles will instinctively try to retard the movement of the planchette and this tendency must be consciously overcome. Just remain as relaxed as possible.

When the experiment is properly performed, the planchette will be moved by psychic energy acting under mental guidance. It is quite possible for your own mind, or that of your companion, to assume this direction, but it is unlikely. Only someone with a fair degree of previous experience can direct a planchette with any degree of success. Occasionally you will find it moving aimlessly about the board which indicates that the energy is there but the mental direction is not. Since most people regard this as some sort of a party game, extremely frivolous results are commonplace. This is to be expected. The emotional and mental attitude of the sitters will attract the interest of other minds on the same level. These may be discarnate intelligences or they may be the minds of living persons that have temporarily wandered away from their bodies, which may be in deep sleep or under the influence of liquor, narcotics or drugs.

Of course there are many people who approach the ouija board in a serious manner and seek from it answers to problems that trouble them. The vast majority of these sincere seekers believe that every reply they receive must come from the mind of a person who has died. They are convinced that the sole cause of planchette movement is direction from *discarnate* (so-called) entities. And because they are no longer in a body their pronunciamentos are accepted as profound truth by these guileless persons. It is important to realize that John Smith dead is no different and no smarter than John Smith alive. He may be more aware of people's motives and he may even be able to see a little ahead in time, but for the most part his knowledge and, more importantly, his judgment is no better than it was while he was "living."

Importance of adequate planning

So if you wish to experiment with a planchette, prepare yourself well. Follow the suggestions given early in this chapter to those interested in automatic writing. Cleanse yourself physically. Seek out a place where you can be alone—or with but one other collaborator—and where you will be safe from interruption and outside distractions. Raise the level of your consciousness by meditation or by reading from an inspirational book. This will enhance your chances for a high-grade, helpful contact, and I hope you will be fortunate enough to make one. If you don't, if the initial replies and statements seem at all confused, ambiguous or frivolous, stop the work immediately.

Even if you are intrigued by some phase of this response—or more important, because you are intrigued by it—drop it. Along this road lies unpleasantness and often mischief. Avoid it. Set aside the board and planchette and do not return to it until another day when you have taken particular pains to properly prepare yourself. Unless you can approach this experiment in a high frame of mind it is better not to try it at all.

The automatic writing is quicker and easier but the average beginner finds it beyond his ability. Nearly everyone can get a ouija board and its accompanying planchette to work and many seekers start in this way. It is unfortunate that lack of proper preparation has led so many to an instinctive revulsion to the contacts made via the ouija board and cut short what might have been a promising development of their inner abilities. As has been pointed out, this need not happen and will not happen if the emotional and mental frame of the sitter is properly purified and raised in advance.

TYPES OF PSYCHIC MEDIUMS

The role of the medium is far better documented in the hundreds of books on spiritualism than can possibly be described in the small space allotted here. There are many types of mediums, classified more or less by their abilities and the type of work they do. Some merely report messages which they alone hear, while others can turn over their physical equipment to the use of another entity so that the very voice itself changes from its normal way of speaking; some can cause objects in the room to move about without physical support, while still others can cause discarnate personalities to appear and speak. All of these manifestations and many others are brought about through psychic energy.

Characteristics of mediums

The outstanding characteristic of a medium is the ability to accumulate and employ a large charge of psychic energy. While originally a medium was considered to be nothing more than the term "medium" implies, that is a connecting link or transfer agent between those in physical bodies and those who are not, it is today quite obvious that almost all mediums manifest psychic powers in many other ways. And in my opinion every medium of any ability can operate in a great number of super-physical ways if he or she but realize it. As in the case of all of us, mediums are frequently limited by their own inhibitions and prejudices. They often ascribe to spirits actions they are quite capable of performing on their own.

A well known pastor of a church of Spiritualism in the East has made certain prophetic statements that in the course of time have proved to be accurate. He credits this prevision to spirit guides, yet this is his own vision. He can and should realize this, and he will if he can clear away the personal humility, a result of early teaching, which blocks him off from a belief that he car really do these things.

Spirit controls

Many mediums have "spirit controls," guides who take over and protect them while the physical body is in a trancelike state. Sometimes these guides are exactly as presumed, discarnate entities who lived many years ago and have now dedicated themselves to aiding in this work. In certain instances there is a different element involved. Several years ago I went with a group to a Spiritual church conducted by a very successful medium. His "guide" would apparently take possession of his body as soon as the trance state was established. His features changed and his voice from a clear tenor became harsh and guttural. The medium, of course, had never seen this personality and knew of him only through the eyes of the sitters who had described him. This guide was extremely competent and businesslike. He radiated authority and conducted the entire seance with efficiency and dispatch. As I observed him I became aware of a certain link or affinity with the medium so, when it came my turn, I asked a question or two concerning the guide himself.

"What is your name and when did you live?" I asked.

"My full name is Set-ix-Antl-ao-Ra but I am known here as Xantho. I lived 7800 years ago," came the deep throated reply.

"Where did you live and how did you receive your training?" was my next question.

"I lived in what is now Egypt and I was trained in this and other arts as a priest in the Temple of Learning and Wisdom."

Then I came to my key question. "What is your connection with _____?" and I mentioned the medium's name.

"He and I are the same," came the surprising answer. "This is now my body."

Many of the people present were startled but I understood him to mean that this powerful entity was but a former incarnation of the present mild mannered medium. I asked for more information which he gave unreservedly. He had acquired great knowledge in that life which he carried over to the next. But then the power that became his worked its corrupting influence and, in spite of all his knowledge, he abused it causing great misery to many. After more than three thousand years in the spirit world during which time he had ample opportunity to review and regret his colossal cruelties, he was finally permitted to start again, this time almost from the bottom, so to speak. His basic knowledge displayed itself life after life as fine instincts and a desire to serve others but his abilities were sealed off from conscious use. The unselfish willingness to serve and help others which shone so brightly in his present life was leading him back and gradually permitting him to recall his once great spiritual powers. He now commands psychic energy in abundance, and before he leaves this life he may come to employ it in many other ways in addition to his mediumship.

APPORTS

Psychic energy cannot of itself be seen but i can be employed to mould and control certain physical and semi-physical substances. Some mediums are capable of generating a subtle substance to which the name "ectoplasm" has been given. Psychic energy shapes this into various forms, at the guidance of the medium or one of his controls, and these "created" objects can be seen by anyone. They are not very durable however and usually disintegrate within a few minutes. This type of manifestation is vastly different from an actual "apport" which involves bringing a physical object into the presence of the medium and the sitters or causing an object in the room to disappear and go somewhere else. There are a great many mediums who are capable of manifesting ectoplasm but only a handful have enough skill and psychic energy to transport a durable physical object from one place to another.

The average person who witnesses an apport usually reacts in one of two ways: he either regards it as a trick, a sleight of hand performance, or he refuses to believe his senses and says it just didn't happen. It is only rarely that you find anyone who will face the obvious with an open mind, accept it as having happened and then seek to find the underlying cause.

I have only witnessed two apports that I could recognize as

such, but I have several times been the "victim" of what were certainly mysterious appearances and disappearances. Of course I have read or heard of many genuine apports and noteworthy among these were the appearance in midair, and the floating down to table or floor, of letters, manuscripts and freshly cut flowers in the presence of Mme. Helena Blavatsky. Once each year, Dr. H. Spencer Lewis, then the head of the Rosicrucians in America, would publicly perform an apport in the presence of three or four hundred witnesses. I was privileged to be present at one of these when a bunch of roses was apported into the center of the room some thirty feet from the platform on which he sat. From the middle of the 19th Century to the present day there have been many psychics and mediums in Europe and America who have demonstrated some truly remarkable and adequately verified apports. But, of course, this skill is far more prevalent in Asia, particularly India, where at the present time, I am assured, there are no less than twenty men and one woman who have publicly performed this feat.

POLTERGEIST PHENOMENA

We cannot leave the subject of apports without discussing one of its most annoying but fascinating aspects, that called poltergeist phenomena. This is a fairly common manifestation. Hardly a week goes by without a report from some part of this country describing stones falling in rooms, pictures being thrown from walls, furniture being moved about and similar disturbances. Here is a characteristic report:

> On the night of July 11, 1966, reports V. M. Windes, and for many nights thereafter, small rocks, typical of the area, racketed against the walls and across the tin roof of the house of Alfares Quintana in Llano, New Mexico. His wife, Mrs. Jane Quintana, complained to the police but despite the nightly vigil the pelting continued. One afternoon the attack began about 4:30 in broad daylight and the stones broke several windows, but no one was ever observed throwing them. Apparently they materialized out of thin air and catapulted themselves against the house.
>
> The Quintana house is on a rise and faces down a slope

to the Santa Barbara River about 1000 yards away. Between the house and the road there are a barn and a corral, with lots of open space. Everyone who has seen the home agrees that it would be impossible to get within rock throwing distance of it without being seen.

The first night or two the Quintanas thought it must have been the work of pranksters or vandals. But when it continued with police equipped with flashlights guarding the exterior, they were forced to seek another explanation. The Quintanas have six children ranging in age from 3 to 17 and all were within the house during each of the bombardments. Three of the children are girls ranging from 8 to 14 and this fact is mentioned because it may be significant. After two weeks the rock throwing stopped and apparently was not resumed, but the cause and the thrower were never discovered.

The foregoing is a fairly characteristic account of what is called a poltergeist phenomenon. The word poltergeist is German and means a "throwing ghost" or a "pelting ghost." In nearly every case that has been investigated it was found that there was a young girl or boy in the family, more often a girl, between the ages of 10 and 15. Where the investigator had a certain amount of psychic sensitivity he was able to trace the activity to the young girl who was always on the scene, but in the background, when the disturbances took place. After a careful study of many cases the conclusion was reached that this was usually the result of a conscious and deliberate wielding of psychic energy in a mischievous manner in an attempt to create excitement and attract attention. Seldom was any harm done but usually many people were mystified, frightened and upset.

It is considered that these young "poltergeists" discover their ability to apport objects quite by accident. Being young their minds turn to mischief rather than constructive work. For a time they are amused and sometimes quite gleeful at the discomfiture of their elders, but this eventually palls, and lacking imagination they become bored and cease it. Usually after a few months of inactivity they forget just how they used their excess psychic energy, they lose the technique and never return to it again.

While no one of the Quintana children has so far admitted being
the cause, it seems fairly certain that one of them was responsible.

I might point out here that every mysterious happening has a
cause, and a cause that can in all probability be related to a
human being. In days gone by, people were very superstitious
and anything not obviously of physical origin was attributed to
angels, devils or ghosts. We have now come to know that 99%
of all such occurrences can be traced to human activity and human
psychic energy. It may be acting in a way not quite understood,
it may be demonstrating something never before observed, but,
believe me, somewhere in the act is a person like yourself who is
supplying the energy if not the actual direction. Many of these
seemingly strange activities are not impossible for you yourself
to perform. You have the ability in either embryonic or latent
form. If latent, you can stimulate it and make it work in a relatively short time; if embryonic, it will take more time and more
work. The point I want to drive home is that every human being
has capacities he does not even dream of. You can do amazing
things if you but set your mind to it. There are no miracles—there
are only things that you have not yet learned. Start now to find out!

9

The Various Ways in Which
Psychic Sensitivity
Manifests

Everyone has some degree of psychic sensitivity. The vast majority never take notice of the impressions they receive or, if they should become aware of the unusual, tend to pass it off under some commonplace label. For example, if such a skeptic, on entering a completely dark room, were to suddenly realize there was someone else there, his inclination would be to ascribe this knowledge to hearing or possibly to his olfactory sense. It is true that either one or both of these faculties may have been responsible but it also happens fairly frequently that some other personal "informer" serves notice of the unexpected presence.

This sort of awareness is usually observed as a tingling on the surface of the skin on the arms and shoulders, or on the neck at the base of the skull. The information in such an event is provided by an extrasensory awareness which translates itself to the physical consciousness through the tactile sense, or sense of touch, when actually no physical contact or touch is involved. Yet there is a "feeling" someone is there.

The medium felt is psychic energy. The energy radiating from the visitor is picked up by one's own psychic receptor apparatus and this creates the "feeling" of presence.

Everyone possesses such equipment but its efficiency varies from person to person. As you train yourself to perform one or more of the experiments described in earlier chapters, as you learn to dowse or to exert a personality influence over others, you will at the same time be refining your psychic senses. The various areas of psychic perception will then become more active and as they do you will have many new and sometimes exciting experiences.

HUNCHES

Everyone has "hunches" although some people do not describe them to themselves in that way. You have a feeling that you should buy a raincoat and the next day there is a downpour. Or you suddenly think you should call your mother who lives in another city and when you make the call, for the first time in more than a month, you discover she is sick and needs help. These two fairly common examples of "hunches" are not in the least the same. They are the result of vastly different psychic functions. The urge to buy a raincoat is stimulated by precognition, the impulse to call your mother by a form of telepathy. The only thing in common to the two is the psychic energy used.

There are many different types of hunches. Usually they fall into one of the two here-mentioned categories, precognition and telepathy. Some people have hunches quite frequently, others seldom or never. Since a hunch is a psychic perception which is not realized as such, it is clear that those who have lots of hunches must have a fairly well developed psychic equipment. Presumably they have done nothing in this life to encourage this development so it must have been acquired in one or more previous existences.

One of the basic laws of life is that you never get something for nothing. True, it may sometimes seem that way but in the long run you get just what you pay for. If you want psychic development—and you should because it is a most valuable asset—you must work for it. Actually, you have probably attained a certain degree of psychic ability in previous lives or you would not be reading this now. The very interest that has led you to study this book, regardless of what it was, indicates a stirring of psychic energy within you, a stirring which would not have taken place unless your psychic faculties were at least partially developed. Today the energies available permit a more rapid growth than ever before. Take advantage of this opportunity, I urge you. Use the suggestions herein given to add new abilities and strengthen old ones. Do not regard this casually. See it for what it is, the possibility of achieving a greatness beyond your wildest dreams.

DREAMS

Next to hunches the most common form of psychic expression is through dreams. Up to the present century, dreams were considered by nearly everyone to be the product of a fertile imagination or an over-filled stomach. Today many of our psychiatrists are experimenting with sleeping people in an endeavor to discover the significance of dreams. They have observed that when the eyeballs beneath the closed lids of a sleeper begin to move about in rapid jerky motions, he is then dreaming. This is described as rapid eyeball motion, or R.E.M. for short. All sorts of tests are made. Researchers check on the duration of dreams; they wake sleepers in the middle of a dream and ask what they were dreaming of; they cut dreams short as soon as they start and try to prevent sleepers from dreaming; in fact everything that occurs to the minds of the various investigators is tried in an effort to find out just what dreams are and why we have them.

Dream case histories

There are many dreams that are nothing more than a reaction to an emotional or physical disturbance. These may all be eventually identified and classified at which time one of the psychiatrists will triumphantly announce that everything about dreams is known. But there are many other dreams which have their origin in the psychic faculties and these will always elude physical measurement and so-called scientific appraisal. Let me cite a few such dreams to illustrate this.

CASE A—MRS. R.E.L., STAMFORD, CONN. REPORTS:

My only son had been killed in an automobile accident at the age of 19 and I grieved greatly at his loss. Three months passed but my heart still felt as though it would break and I cried most of the day. In an effort to distract me, my husband suggested we drive to Florida for a week or two and I agreed. Some former neighbors named Whitmire who had a son about the same age as our Bobby had moved to Raleigh, N. C. and since it was on our way we decided to visit them.

On the way we stopped overnight in a motel in Virginia and during the night I had a dream in which Bobby came and talked with me. He looked fine and healthy and he seemed to be standing right in front of me in a white sort of light. He said, "Mama, I am all right and I feel fine so I want you to stop crying. You'll only make yourself sick. I'm just as alive as I ever was, more so maybe, so there is nothing for you to feel sorry about."

I must have registered some sort of incredulity because he said then:

"I see I have to prove this to you. Tomorrow when you get to the Whitmires, Charley won't be there. He is working in Washington in the Federal recording office. Mr. Whitmire has had a stroke and you will find him in bed. Tomorrow when you get to Raleigh you will see this is true and you are not just imagining this. I love you, mama, and I don't want you to make yourself sick, particularly for no reason."

With that he disappeared and the light seemed to dim. Suddenly I realized I was in strange surroundings. When I became aware that I was in bed in a motel and had just awakened from a beautiful dream, I woke my husband and told him all about it. He told me I had been dreaming and I accepted this until we arrived in Raleigh about noon the next day and found Mr. Whitmire in bed as described and Charley away in Washington.

CASE B—A.E.S. BRONX, N.Y. REPORTS:

Some years ago when I was working as a railway mail clerk on the New York-Boston run of the New Haven R.R., I had a side-kick and pal named Gus. He and I worked this run for three or four years and usually spent our away-from-home breaks together. So I knew him pretty well.

One night I had a very bad dream, a real nightmare, and I awoke in a cold sweat. I must have made some noise because my wife woke too and asked me if I was all right. I was still shaking so I lit the light and a cigarette and told her about it. Sometimes it's good to get something like that off your chest.

I dreamt I was in the back seat of a car, Gus's car. He and his wife, Mary, were in the front seat and he was driving. Driving? Racing I should say, he was going so fast. Mary kept trying to get him to slow down but he wouldn't pay any attention to her. I then realized he was drunk and tried to talk to him but I couldn't say anything. I made my mouth go but no sounds came out. I recognized where we were, on the Boston Post Road in the Bronx just south of Pelham, and Gus was driving toward New York.

He wouldn't slow down and seemed to go faster. Suddenly a long truck started to pull out of a side street ahead of us. I tried to yell to Gus to stop and I guess he either heard me or saw it because he put his foot on the brake and veered a little to the left. The truck was old and moving slowly across the road from left to right and it began to look like he might miss it when out of no place a car coming toward us on the Post Road hit the truck. There were wheels and glass and bodies and fenders and pieces of wood flying in all directions and we crashed right into the middle of it. The car folded up. Mary flew out the side door onto the road and Gus smacked his head into the windshield. At this point I woke up, shaking.

I asked my wife to call Gus and Mary but there was no answer. It was 1:30 A.M. They should have been home. My wife said, "Stop worrying and go back to sleep. They have a right to stay out if they want to. They're married." So I put out the light and stayed awake until about three o'clock when I dropped off.

The next day I found out there had been an accident and it had happened pretty much just as I had seen it. Gus was a little steamed up and he had been driving too fast. Mary tried to slow him down with no success. There was another couple in the back seat (not me) and Gus was miffed because they had insisted on going home and he wanted to stay at the party. So he was outvoted but resentful and he took it out on the car. The truck had pulled across in front of them, as I had seen it, and it looked as if they could miss it by passing behind it when the car going the other way crashed into it and spread everything all over the road. Mary broke her collar bone and Gus had his head split open but no real damage. The people in back, a young couple my wife and I knew, were only shaken up. The car, the truck and the car going the other way were all pretty badly smashed. Fortunately no one was killed but the driver of the other car ended up in the hospital with two fractured ribs and a broken leg.

Now, how did I dream that almost exactly the way it happened? And I guess at the same time as it happened, too, but I never did check that out exactly.

Case C—A.R.J., Santa Clara, California reports:

I am a research chemist and I work for one of the large west coast manufacturers of space age equipment. My group had been assigned a project which was to develop a metal or an alloy which would be resistant to extremes of both heat and cold. We had been experimenting with several different combinations but had not been able to turn out a satisfactory product. We made one highly resistant to heat and a different one which would retain its durability in great cold but were unable to combine the two virtues.

One night I had a strange dream. I seemed to be in a classroom listening to a lecture. There were others present sitting at desks, as I was, but I took no notice of them. My attention was riveted on the lecturer who seemed to be a man of about 50 with grey hair and a slight build. I did not see his face because he kept it turned toward a blackboard which he filled with figures as he talked. I don't remember a word he said except that it made sense to me, but the figures he wrote remain etched in my memory. For he wrote equations which were very familiar to me. They covered certain phases of the work which I had been struggling with the previous week. But they were not exactly the same; the symbol for silicon, a mineral not previously considered, appeared in several places and with it were certain quantitative notations.

When he concluded his explanation, the instructor started to turn towards myself and the others sitting there, but as he did I suddenly woke up in my bed. But the blackboard and its helpful equations seemed clear in my memory and I hastened to get paper to put them down. The next day at the plant I tested the (to me) new idea suggested by the equations and found the result to be an alloy with most of the desired characteristics. It is now in use.

I have no idea how I happened to dream of a solution to the problem which faced me, but a solution it proved to be, and a good one.

Analysis of the dreams

All three of these dreams have one thing in common. They are all psychic dreams or psychic experiences. But they are not all alike. The psychic function which activated each is entirely different from the other two. Let me explain.

In *Case A* Mrs. R.E.L. was contacted by her son. This contact was not on the physical level. There are several different ways in which this connection might have been established and it is impossible to say which particular technique was employed. But psychic energy supplied by Mrs. R.E.L. was used either at her son's direction or the direction of some more advanced mind who was helping him. Since he had not been dead very long it was probably the latter. Practice and some experience is required to manipulate psychic energy regardless of whether you occupy a physical body or have only its astral counterpart to work with, in other words whether you are what we call dead or you are still alive. It is unlikely that any recently deceased person could acquire this skill in less than a year or two.

In *Case B* A.E.S. experienced what is called astral travel. A part of him, a part which had visual and auditory awareness of its surroundings, left his body and for some reason was drawn to the car driven by his friend, Gus. He actually saw and heard all that occurred leading to and during the accident and was able to recall it fairly accurately when he awoke. People frequently leave their bodies when sleeping but only rarely do they have any waking memories of their experiences in that state. The impressions

received in the so-called astral state are extremely/evanescent. ﾉ
They usually have the permanence of a writing on the surface of
a pool of water. In order that they be recalled in the waking state
psychic energy must be used to write or imprint these impressions
on the physical brain as they occur. This is brought about sometimes by emotional tension, sometimes the higher self will order
it done for a specific reason or it may be done by a highly developed person who wishes to teach a lesson or in some other way
be of help. But even when an imprint is made on the physical
brain and memory, it will vanish quickly, usually within five minutes, if it is not written down or told to someone. The conscious
act of telling or writing makes its own imprint on the brain and
this lasts. So it then becomes the memory of the writing or the
telling that you retain.

Case C is different again. A.R.T. had a problem and he gave
it a great deal of thought. He even took it to bed with him, so to
speak. The result is not at all unusual but the way in which it
presented itself to his conscious mind was unique. Many people,
both deliberately and probably more often without meaning to,
turn problems over to their so-called subconscious to solve. The
word "subconscious" is usually employed to describe this type of
experience but it is inaccurate. The word *superconscious* would
be nearer the truth because it is necessary for the mind to move
up to the third level, the inspirational and creative level, to find
the solution. You usually have no recollection of this. Instead your
thoughts on waking turn in a seemingly idle fashion to the puzzle
you had taken to bed and at that moment there is a flash or an
idea which completely clarifies it. This is the way solutions usually
come to people with modest psychic development. Those more
highly trained and those with greater psychic energy will often
recall the actual experience on the third level but translate it into
some familiar association when bringing it into conscious awareness. This is what happened to A.R.T. The classroom atmosphere
was familiar to him. He had often received instruction under similar circumstances in school and college. Furthermore since the
equations were lengthy and complex, the blackboard was the
simplest way to record them visually so they would remain long

enough in his consciousness for him to write them down—which he fortunately did.

Separating meaningful from meaningless dreams

The subject of dreams is vast and so very complicated that many volumes would be required to even begin to do justice to it. By far the greater percentage of all dreams are meaningless, hopeless jumbles of recollected fragments, imagined story sequences and emotional urges. But there are hundreds of dreams that either wholly or in part are psychically inspired. These are usually more vivid and more reasonable, more purposeful you might say. If you make a practice of writing down your dreams each morning on waking, you will soon be able to separate the meaningful from the inconsequential. Don't wait until after breakfast. By then the memory will have thinned out or disappeared entirely. Write them as soon as you awake and keep them for reading at a later date. They are frequently much more understandable after a month or two.

Many people have warnings in dreams and many see things in dreams that actually happen in the future just as they saw them. These precognitive experiences are usually called premonitions or advance warnings. We will discuss them in the next chapter.

10

How Psychic Energy Can Bring You Premonitions and Help You Become Clairvoyant

There are many different evidences of psychic sensitivity. Most common are hunches and dreams; these have been discussed. Today many people report premonitions of various kinds, some describe experiences of clairvoyance and clairaudience and a few individuals here and there display psychometric skill. Each involves a certain type of psychic activity which I will describe and explain.

PREMONITIONS

A premonition is an advance warning, usually of impending danger. I dare say everyone has had a premonition at one time or another and some people have them fairly frequently. Premonitions are not all alike. They show themselves in various ways and they may come about as the result of any one of many widely differing causes. Let me give you some actual examples of premonition, no two of which are the same.

Case A

Mary Elizabeth, age 8, and her brother Billy, age 5, were playing in a sand bank near their home in Mattawan, New Jersey.

Suddenly Mary heard an urgent voice call, "Bittsy, you and Billy get out of that sand bank right away! Quick now!"

Without a second's thought Mary climbed out of the hole she and her brother had dug and dragged the reluctant Billy after her. They had taken barely three steps away from the "cave" they were digging when the entire bank collapsed and dropped two or three tons of sand right where they had been.

Mary looked to see who had called but there was no one in sight. Returning home she asked her Aunt Elizabeth, who had kept house for them since her mother's death, if she had called.

"It sounded just like you, Aunt Elizabeth," she explained, "but you called me Bittsy and you always call me Mary or Mary Elizabeth."

"No one but your mother and father ever called you Bittsy and I certainly didn't," said her aunt. And then she asked, "What were you doing?"

When she heard the child's description of the collapse of the sand bank she went to see for herself. It was clear that if the children had not gotten out of the hole in time they would have been crushed and killed. Again she asked the children what they had heard. Billy had heard nothing and said so. Mary Elizabeth repeated that it had sounded like her aunt's voice and she assumed it had been her aunt calling.

The aunt knew better. She had not called. In fact she had not been out of the house which was below the hill and out of sight of the sand bank. But she knew she and her sister Mary had voices that were much alike and frequently one had been mistaken for the other. Yet Mary had been dead for four years. It was a sobering thought.

It is clear what took place. The mother, still concerned for her children's safety and aware of the imminent collapse of the sand bank, mentally employed the psychic energy of her daughter to warn her. The warning reached the consciousness of the little girl like urgently spoken words. Yet they were not audible, for the brother heard nothing. This form of premonition is not unusual. A person, alive or dead, aware of impending danger, uses the psychic energy of the one threatened and impresses him (or her) in the most effective way possible to take the necessary action to avoid it. This is one kind of premonition.

Case B

Here now is a different type. H.E.S., New York, N. Y. reports:

I dreamed one night that I was in a strange office building. As I went to enter the elevator, the operator's face changed to a grinning skull. Frightened, I stepped back, and the dream ended.

Two days later while on a call on the 12th floor of an old building I noticed while waiting for the elevator that the hall seemed vaguely familiar. At that moment the elevator door opened and as I started to get in I looked at the operator. Amazingly his face changed just as in my dream. Instead of a pleasant smiling countenance I found myself looking into the vacant eye sockets of a skull. This startled me so, I stepped back just as I had in my dream. The door closed and the elevator went down. But it didn't stop as it should. The supporting cable broke and it fell the entire 12 stories and landed with a great crash in the basement. The operator and the two passengers were seriously injured but I was spared. By what?

This man was saved by his own precognition. His psychic awareness saw the possibility of danger two days in advance and sought to warn his conscious mind. The connection was not too good and he brought back only part of the warning which he did not understand. It was necessary therefore that it be repeated immediately before the accident.

Here is a case where the psychic mind, the superconscious mind, or the cosmic mind (it has many names) used a most ingenious device to bring a warning to this man's attention. For a fraction of a second, it gave him the illusion of looking at a human skull instead of a normal face and this startled him just enough to cause him to step away from the doomed elevator.

Analysis of premonitions

We have seen here two different kinds of premonition, one in which a dead mother, concerned for the safety of her children, was successful in reaching the mind of her daughter with a warning. The other was a case of precognition by a man who has definite psychic ability but is unaware of it. In this case he was startled in a dramatic manner into taking the step which saved him from certain injury and possibly death. Both types are quite common.

There are literally hundreds of recorded cases of each and who knows how many more that have never been spoken of. It is unfortunate that people are so self-conscious and timid about relating experiences which are out of the ordinary. Of course they fear incredulity and possibly ridicule. Yet today, if they but realized it, they are very apt to find a sympathetic and understanding audience, for thousands have had psychic experiences of their own and others have read or heard the statements of credible witnesses.

Another form of premonition

Quite often a premonition will take the form of a sudden "like" or "dislike," a feeling that you want to do a thing on the one hand or violently oppose it on the other. A good example of this is the case reported by Gladys Guyne in the November 1967 issue of *Fate Magazine.**

> When she was about 10 years old Gladys Guyne and her father started one day to go from their home to the center of the city where they lived. Their house was on one of the hills surrounding the town and the business section was down in the valley. The electric trolley car was the normal means of transportation and this they intended to take.
> When the car came to a stop before them and they were about to board it, little Gladys suddenly became terrified and

* Naomi Groat, "The Trolley," *Fate Magazine,* November 1967, p. 60.

refused to enter. She cried, "Please, Daddy, can't we walk? I want to walk. I don't want to get on the car."

To avoid a scene her father gave in and they started to walk. Twenty minutes later, when they came to the bottom of the long hill and approached the retail store section of the town, they came upon the very car lying on its side. The brakes had failed and it had plunged down the hill at increasing speed until it ran off the track and turned over. Everyone on the car was seriously injured and some were crippled for life.

When questioned, Gladys Guyne said she had no idea why she had refused to ride on the car. She was only 10 years old and all she could say was "I just didn't want to get on the horrid old car."

This is a perfect example of a premonition working through a feeling of dislike, or "not want," and it is very common. The individual possesses psychic energy and has precognitive ability but no understanding of it. It seems likely that for every warning of this kind that is heeded, there are hundreds that are shrugged off. From this you can realize how important it is for you to develop your psychic faculties and acquire the psychic energy needed for them to function at top efficiency.

CLAIRVOYANCE

Clairvoyance is the ability to see on the etheric and astral levels, normally well beyond the capacity of physical sight. Clairaudience is the ability to hear sounds, usually voices, that are not audible to the average human ear. Clairvoyance and clairaudience are often referred to as "lower psychic faculties." This same designation is applied to hunches, psychic dreams and the ability to psychometrize. All of these remarkable abilities are evidence of a sensitivity to psychic energy as it functions on the astral and etheric levels. A person may be completely aware on the astral plane and be able to move about in that subtle world with surprising freedom and never rise higher. Yet there are far greater and more important realms above and beyond the astral which await discovery.

The veil between physical and etheric levels

If we refer back to the simile used in an earlier chapter, we may consider our existence, our entire being, as a house with several levels. Everyone is aware of the ground floor level. This is the normal physical world and the people in it. The second level, the next floor higher, is the level of the astral world, sometimes called the emotional world. Between the two there is an intermediate level, almost like a balcony over the ground floor level, that manifests characteristics of both. This is usually called the etheric or energy level. Today mystics say that the veil between the physical and etheric levels is getting very thin. This is a symbolical way of indicating that there is more psychic energy pouring into humanity than ever before and that this energy is stimulating into activity previously unknown and undeveloped faculties in thousands of people. I am endeavoring in this book to familiarize you with a few of the many ways in which these abilities work. And I am also indicating methods by which you, if you will, can learn more about your own capacities and how to develop them.

It is unquestionably true that as a man nears perfection, all of his faculties are brought into play. But this is not a simultaneous occurrence. Each is developed by itself as attention is focussed upon it. In the chapter on inspiration I pointed out that the dedicated musician found his inspiration in that realm and not in painting, while the architect who sought and acquired additional psychic energy found ideas for monuments and buildings flowing into him, not poetry. As great quantities of energy are brought into action it is inevitable that the development of more than one set of faculties will take place. Leonardo da Vinci was not only a painter of genius but he was also a great inventor, hundreds of years ahead of his time. In our day Nicholas Roerich, probably the outstanding artist of the 20th century, was also a talented writer, a remarkable orator and a most discerning and successful archaeologist. However, as a journey of one hundred miles must start with the first step, so it is that in the development of your psychic abilities it is necessary to concentrate first on one to the exclusion of the others. The distinctions between them are given here and the more common are briefly described so that you will

not make the error of assuming, as so many do, that all are alike
and that if you know one you know all.

The psychic faculty of inspiration

It might be well to point out here that inspiration is one of the
so-called higher psychic faculties. Using once again our clumsy
simile of a house with many stories, we can say that inspiration is
found on the third level. Here psychic energy works with the
mind. The emotions, when they enter at all, are used as tools
or instruments of the mind. On the third level are to be found
not only the inspiration so necessary to human advancement but
also the visions of the future which are identified as true prophecy.
To reach this level in consciousness requires deep understanding,
a well defined technique and confidence. The attainment of these
will be described in the chapters on projection. But here we will
continue with our examination of the lower psychic faculties and
consider next the ability to register, as sight, impressions coming
from the etheric or astral levels. This is called clairvoyance or
"clear seeing."

How clairvoyance functions on the etheric level

We take the mechanics of our physical sight for granted. Yet
it would require the combined knowledge of an eye specialist and
a psychiatrist to describe the intricate process by which impressions reach the brain when the eye sees something. Psychic vibrations manifest visually in a very simple manner, but it is even
more difficult to explain this process to one who has not actually
experienced it. Possibly an example, a case history, will help you
to understand how clairvoyance functions on the etheric level.

Mrs. G.M. is the widow of a very wealthy man. At one time
she occupied a position of prominence in the social world and
it was said that an invitation to her home was the guarantee
of social status. Today she spends most of her time working
in hospitals and clinics as a medical assistant, a most unusual
assistant to two doctors. She has no medical degree and, in
fact, not even elementary nurse's training, yet she has a certain exceptional talent which these two medical men are
putting to use. Here is an example of how she works:

Dr. A had a patient who complained of chronic headaches and he decided to get Mrs. M's impressions. He asked her to stop at his office at the time of the patient's next appointment and when she arrived he told her, "My patient is in the other room. I have told her I want her to walk around for a few minutes to stimulate her heart action. This will give you an opportunity to look at her from every angle while you sit there as if waiting for me to be free. Go in there now. In two or three minutes I will summon my patient and then when she has gone we can discuss what you have observed."

A half hour later, when Dr. A and Mrs. M. were once again alone in his office, he asked impatiently, "What did you see? Anything unusual?"

"I don't think there is anything seriously wrong with this woman," Mrs. M. reported. "The energy vortex at her throat is a little more active than it normally should be and there are flashes of red in it that do not belong there. However I believe this may be an effect and not a cause. It seems to me the problem in this case may be the intestines. They are too dark in color and the energy cones are sluggish and slightly erratic in their vibratory motion. It appears to me she may need some sort of an intestinal stimulant, something to speed up their activity."

Dr. A thanked her and stated he had scheduled the patient for a gastro-intestinal x-ray examination the following day and would also make other tests. Later he told Mrs. M. that his own study of the patient had confirmed the appraisal she had made in three or four minutes. His painstaking and thorough examinations took ten days and might have taken longer had he not had the observations of Mrs. M. to guide him.

As you observe, Dr. A is open-minded and willing to employ unconventional methods to aid his patients. His treatment in this case was interesting. He employed medication as a temporary relief only and soon discontinued it. His basic prescription was exercise, a daily work-out for the waist and abdominal area. This not only brought an increased supply of blood to the intestines and associated organs but it strengthened the entire abdominal corset. The patient was relieved of her headaches and today, two years later, they have not recurred.

Etheric Vision

Mrs. G.M. has excellent etheric vision. She discovered this quite by accident and because she did not understand what she experienced, she confided in Doctor L., one of the two men with whom she presently works. It was his, and her, great good fortune that he understood the nature of her gift. When she chooses, the whole energy structure of the person before her becomes visible. She sees the rapidly spinning wheels and cones of light vibrating at different rates in different colors. At first this was a meaningless jumble but with the help of Dr. L. she learned the medical, surgical and physiological significance of what she saw. Today she is a skilled diagnostician, and in fact these two men depend quite heavily upon her observations. They never accept her vision alone but always check most carefully in all ways available to them. In many cases though she has been able to point out physical weaknesses that might not have been discovered for a year or more had the doctors not tested for them at her suggestion.

The clairvoyance of Mrs. M. works most effectively on the physical and etheric levels. I mention physical because she has recently expanded her remarkable ability in a most unusual way. With the guidance of her two medical co-workers, she has trained herself to look "into" the physical body itself and understand what she sees. This is another amazing gift of psychic energy, a faculty which will be studied and consciously developed in the medical schools of tomorrow. Mrs. M. can look into the internal organs of the body and actually see and recognize any malfunction or breakage that may exist. This is a forerunner of the medical diagnosis of the future. Many already have this ability to some degree but do not understand it. They should be sought out and their natural clairvoyance trained to a point where it may be usefully employed. Enough time has already been wasted. Let us now endeavor to apply psychic energy to practical good!

Normally, Mrs. M. does not have astral vision, although among clairvoyants this is far more common. She is conscious, of course, of emotional stresses because she can see the energy patterns change under emotional pressure, but she does not ordinarily observe the shifting emotional colorations themselves. Yet almost every individual capable of clairvoyant vision functions on the astral level. This is for most people the area of greatest interest. Nearly all of us are emotionally focussed and energy flows in the greatest volume to where our attention sends it. Thus by far the greatest number of people capable of clairvoyance will register the astral, and thousands of examples can be given.

Emotions may trigger clairvoyant experience

You yourself, or someone you know, may have had a clairvoyant experience. When this occurs to the average unaware and untrained individual (which is to say one lacking occult knowledge and experience), it usually comes about as the result of some strong emotional stimulus or tension. A relative dies and a few nights later you are awakened from a sound sleep to see this same relative standing near your bed. He looks young, strong and healthy. There is a shine in his eyes and, if he speaks, his voice is firm and strong. Sometimes there is a message, sometimes just the visual is experienced.

This form of clairvoyance is very common. The initiating drive is emotional, a certain emotional tension in the living person, which is the natural result of the loss of a person known and possibly loved, plus a desire on the part of the departed soul to reassure his friends and loved ones that he still exists and is happier and stronger than heretofore. The living person supplies the psychic energy and the departed one provides the thought form which, by employing the tools of desire or wishfulness, fashions that psychic energy into a visible image. Here is an actual experience which will illustrate this.

> Arthur S. and his sister Betty had lived together in the family home until she married Harold, who had been a friend of both from childhood. After the wedding Arthur continued to live in the old house while Betty and Harold had a new house built in another part of the city. Arthur and Betty were both open-minded on the question of human survival. Neither had any firm convictions and frankly stated that they just didn't know. Harold, on the other hand, was a materialist. He scoffed at the idea of an afterlife and said more than once, "When you're dead, you're dead. It's final."

After ten years of happy married life, Harold was stricken with a heart ailment and died quite suddenly. Arthur suggested to Betty that she return to the old home and live there as she had before her marriage. But she felt a sentimental attachment to the home which she and Harold had built and where she had spent so many happy years. She recognized the definite advantages of a joint menage, not the least of which were the economies effected and the companionship offered. But sentiment and possibly pride in her own home decided her against the change.

One night, about four months after Harold's death, Arthur woke suddenly with the feeling that someone had called his name. The room was silent but standing in the doorway to the hall was Harold. Arthur could see him distinctly, "in full color," as he afterwards said, although there was no light on in the room. He looked young and healthy, just about as he had looked when he was married ten years before.

When he was certain he had Arthur's attention he spoke, "I want you to tell Betty," he started to say but at this point the voice faded into inaudibility, his appearance became misty and he disappeared.

Convinced he had been dreaming Arthur turned over and was soon asleep. He did not know how long afterward he was awakened again. This time he felt someone holding his right arm and shaking him. When he finally roused himself he saw Harold standing near the right side of his bed, completely visible as before.

Again Harold spoke and said, "I want you to tell Betty I think she should move back here. I know you have already suggested it, but tell her I would like her to. She can sell our house and make a good profit if she acts before summer."

Arthur started to ask how he could convince Betty that Harold wanted this, but before he could speak his visitor continued, "She will need the deed. It is not in the safe deposit with the other papers but in an envelope in the middle left hand drawer of my desk. Tell her."

Having said this he disappeared quite suddenly without fading into a mist as in the first appearance. Arthur reported all this to Betty and, when she found the deed where Harold had said it was, she was convinced it was his wish for her to move back with her brother.

Clairvoyant experience produced by psychic energy

It is clear from the foregoing that it was the strong desire of Harold to advise his wife which created the conditions of the clairvoyant experience. Arthur had no previous experience and was not even interested in the mystical or occult. Yet he has what is known as a magnetic personality so it is quite probable that it was his psychic energy which was employed to make the body of Harold visible and his voice audible. This was a new experience for Harold, too, as is evidenced by the initial failure and the need for a second effort. One can almost imagine him being instructed in what to do and how to do it when his concern for his wife's well-being led him to want to communicate with her.

The trained clairvoyant finds it possible to "see" on the astral plane almost at will. I use the word "almost" because there are occasions when this skill is dulled and fails to function with normal efficiency. Arthur Ford in this country and John Pendragon in England, although quite different personally, are two of many well known mediums who can function clairvoyantly at will. Mediumistic powers and clairvoyance do not always coincide in a person, but in highly developed individuals this is often the case.

The Reverend Arthur Ford has been consulted many times by scientists endeavoring to obtain evidence of survival after death. On one such occasion he said to the investigator, "There is a young man standing next to you. He has his hand on your shoulder." To the puzzled seeker, who could see and feel nothing out of the ordinary, this statement smacked of charlatanry. He just could not believe it and naturally concluded the clairvoyant was "making it up." After this initial rejection, all evidence offered was either refused entirely or received with skepticism. Yet the Reverend Ford actually saw the young man and proceeded to describe accurately the appearance of the dead son of the investigator. This scientist is not to be criticized. We have all come to depend so thoroughly on the reports brought to our consciousness by our five physical senses that it requires a very open mind to accept the fact that there are some who have sensory equipment transcending the physical. What is even more surprising to the average man is the information that he himself possesses this equipment and can with practice learn to use it.

HOW TO IMPROVE CLAIRVOYANT ABILITY

Here is a simple exercise which I urge you to perform. Do it as often as you can, several times a day if possible. Only good can come from it.

1. Sit in a comfortable but relaxed position and close your eyes.
2. Place the ball of the forefinger of each hand on the closed lid of the corresponding eye so that it rests directly over the pupil.
3. Hold this position while you take three deep breaths, retaining each as long as possible before exhaling.
4. While holding your breath, visualize your head and shoulders surrounded by a brilliant white cloud of shimmering psychic energy.
5. As you exhale, feel this energy run down your arms and out the tips of your index fingers into your eyes. Be careful that you do not press upon your eyes. Just touch your finger tips lightly to the closed lids so that the eyeball has free movement at all times.

Let me repeat. Perform this simple exercise whenever you can, several times each day if possible. The psychic energy thus directly delivered to your eyes will bring both physical and psychic benefits. It will strengthen your eye muscles and increase the sensitivity of the optic nerves. Thus you will find your physical sight improving. Many people, long accustomed to the need for glasses, have found that after a few months of practice their sight had so improved that glasses were no longer required. Not so immediate, but in the long run more important, will be a gradual reawakening of your latent clairvoyant ability. At first you will detect movement out of the corner of your eye which will disappear when faced directly. Next you will observe shadows where none should exist. Finally actual forms will become visible which should so encourage you that you will work for, and achieve, a complete clairvoyance.

11

How Psychic Energy Can Help You Develop Clairaudience and Psychometry Powers

Surprising as it may seem, almost everyone is capable of so-called super-physical awareness to some degree. Because the physical impacts upon our senses are so powerful, the more subtle reports usually go unnoticed. Even when there is a slight breakthrough into consciousness the gentle touch or sound is ignored more often than not. Most people are clairaudient, which is to say they can, and frequently do, hear sounds on a level above the physical. The average human ear registers sounds between 50 and 12,000 cycles per second. Children, some trained musicians and certain animals can identify sounds between 15,000 and 20,000 cycles, a range in which most people find silence.

The subtle impressions which are picked up by a clairaudient are really not sounds at all, at least not sound as it is conventionally understood. They are vibrations, yes, but in a very high range which is all they have in common with ordinary everyday sounds.

They impress the consciousness of the listener as sounds but this is because he has trained his sense of awareness to step down these extremely high vibratory impacts to a level where his brain can record them. This is a learned ability; it is the result of a conscious effort to know, made either in this life or a previous life, and focussed on an auditory interpretation.

CLAIRAUDIENCE A COMMON PSYCHIC SENSE

The reason why clairaudience is the most common psychic sense needs some explaining. I will now tell you the reason why this is so and give you a technique which will enable you to recall and renew this ability if you have it within you, or if you have not, to develop it now for the first time.

Many thousands of years ago (I hesitate to say how many for fear of arousing incredulity) there were two basic classes of human beings. There were those who were pretty much as we in the western world are today—intelligent, well-formed, good looking and healthy. This upper class comprised many different races, and those with skins of a bluish tan and a reddish bronze color were in greatest numbers. They ruled the planet and regarded themselves as the only human beings. The others were regarded as "things," not human beings. These "things" were stupid, with awkward and misshapen bodies which often displayed animal characteristics like tails and horns. Small wonder the "humans" regarded them with contempt and used them as slaves. But these "things" were actual human beings who had not yet developed and eventually were recognized as such and treated accordingly. But this was many thousands of years later, almost in modern times.

The "humans," in addition to superior intelligence, had many other qualities and abilities not enjoyed by the "things." One was the capacity for telepathic contact with each other when necessary. Since the "things" had no concept of what this was, let alone the ability to practice it, you can see what a big advantage it gave the "humans." These "things" outnumbered the "humans" many times over and, as was natural, they on occasion sought to take advantage of their numerical superiority to win power. But the telepathic ability of the "humans" enabled them to bring instant help, help which usually came bearing mind-searing weapons against which the "things" had no defense. Thus these sub-human beings were kept in subjugation and used as slaves for many thousands of years.

IMPORTANCE OF TELEPATHIC UNDERSTANDING

You can see from this how important it was for every "human" to develop the ability to send and receive telepathic messages. Not every one of the "humans" was born a competent telepath, although most were. Those who did not display this competence by their seventh year were then given a course of training designed to awaken psychic energy and stimulate the centers involved. Since this course was for the training of little children, boys and girls from seven to ten years of age, it is really quite simple. I will explain it to you so you can train yourself, if you wish. It usually took the children about three years to become as competent with *mental* speech as they were with the spoken word. If you have known this before, and there is a good possibility you have, it will not take you that long because, as you see, you will not be learning something entirely new but recalling what has been already learned in the forgotten past.

An experiment in clairaudience

You will need the assistance of another who may or may not be told what you are doing, as you wish. Let me say once again, before giving you this technique, that it is very simple, but do not let this deceive you. It works very well and has for thousands of years. Now here is a modern version, not the same obviously but just as effective. This is what you are to do.

1. Get a book of verse or poems, preferably one with four-line verses that have rhythm and rhyme.
2. Find a fairly secluded place where you are not apt to be interrupted or disturbed by outside noises for about 15 minutes.
3. Seat yourself comfortably in a relaxed position and ask your collaborator to sit a few feet away, facing in another direction from you.

4. Have your collaborator select a short verse at random and read it through once.
5. Then have him read it a line at a time, while you repeat the line he has read after him, before he goes on to the next line. Do this three times.
6. The fourth time he should read the first three lines with you, repeating them as before, but have him stop after the third line and read the fourth to himself silently.
7. You should endeavor to say the line aloud as he reads it silently or after he has finished. Do not be elated if you do this—do not be disappointed if you fail. This is only a training exercise.
8. Then go to another poem. It need not be of only four lines. Any short poem or stanza of a poem will do. But it should not be over six lines in length. Beyond this the reading becomes too lengthy and unwieldy.
9. Go from verse to verse and continue this exercise for no more than 15 to 30 minutes.

This may seem more like a memory exercise than a training in telepathy. In the beginning it may be entirely memory but as you proceed from verse to verse, never repeating, you will gradually come to realize that there is another factor coming into play. You will seem to hear your collaborator's voice even though he is silent. *This is the beginning of the development of your clairaudient faculty.*

Try to find a collaborator who is "sympatico," a person you like, who likes you and is willing to help you. A reluctant collaborator, or one who harbors any dislike or resentment, is valueless. Re member, you are actually going to try to pick up a telepathic message from your collaborator whether he or she be apprised of it or not. So it is important that a certain degree of harmony exist between you. When you have developed skill and power, a previous rapport is not essential, but at first it is necessary.

Do not expect immediate success. And when some evidence appears, by all means continue your training. The average person will require two or three months of daily practice to stir the inner faculties into activity If you should get results earlier, it is a sure indication you are already partly awakened. By going from one verse to another, choosing a new and different one each time, you cut down the possibility of memory being the sole factor. You can also reduce the reading from four to three times and then from three to two. At this point you will have heard the line aloud only once before attempting to repeat it. Your collaborator can also vary the procedure by silently reading the second or third line instead of the last. This he should do unexpectedly, without warning you, in order to achieve maximum benefit.

Gradually you yourself will come to realize that you have clairaudient ability. Encourage this new-found faculty. You will begin to hear sounds and voices not in the normal physical range. Try to pick them up. Show an interest. Where your interest lies, there your energy goes, and this is one excellent way of developing your psychic energy.

A word of caution

Now, a word of caution. As you gain skill and proficiency, you will hear many different voices. It is not necessary that you listen to all. Some sounds may be helpful, others quite the opposite. Learn to choose. It is just as easy, you will find, to shut out unwanted companions on the astral level as it is on the physical. A firm decision on your part is all that is needed.

There are many intelligences seeking a contact, a mouthpiece on the physical level. These are not all discarnate spirits, the astral bodies of people who have died, as might be assumed. They come from many levels, for the astral world is far larger and more varied than the physical. So be choosy. Some may try to flatter you in order to monopolize your attention. Avoid these as a plague. Others, quite well meaning, may try to guide your every physical decision. Do not let them! This is your life you are living, not theirs, and you are held solely responsible for every thought, word and action. Of course there will be occasional warnings of danger and, when one is received, it is well to explore all possibilities involved. The following true incident may explain what I mean.

A warning about a plane obeyed

A former Eastern Airlines official was on a National Airlines plane bound for Miami. As they were flying over Georgia he heard a voice say distinctly in his ear, "Get off the plane at Tampa. There will be trouble later." That was all, and it was not repeated.

His first reaction was that someone had leaned over his shoulder and spoken to him, but a quick glance around convinced him it could not have happened that way. He was still musing over this odd experience when the huge jet touched down at the Tampa Airport. Being a capable and intelligent executive he decided quickly on a course of action.

He went immediately to the office of the airport manager, identified himself and said, "I have received information there may be some trouble on this flight after it leaves Tampa. I have no idea what the nature of the trouble may be, but I think it would be wise if you and the National Airline's officials took extra precautions."

The airport manager accepted this advice as seriously as it was given. He knew the man's reputation and considered him no fool. Also he had his own idea of what form this "trouble" might take. So he ordered the flight delayed and a complete mechanical inspection of the plane before it would be permitted to leave the ground. Also, since several planes had been "hijacked" by Cuban nationals in the past year, he decided to do what he could to cover this possibility as well.

All the passengers who were on the plane were asked to leave and go into a special waiting room while the big jet was being checked over. In the same room were assembled the passengers who were about to board at Tampa on the way to Miami. A stewardess was assigned to check each passenger for name and boarding point.

After going through the room and speaking to everyone, she reported the following to the airport manager, "Most of the passengers seem innocent enough. However there are five men with unusual names and heavy accents and three are boarding here."

The manager felt it would be necessary to search these men, but was unable to think of a way in which it could be done without arousing the passengers' resentment and probably provoking a lawsuit against National Airlines

At this point one of the airport police, who in his younger days had been a detective on the Tampa police force, offered a suggestion. "I have had lots of experience in frisking people," he said. "If you can arrange for these men to pass by me in a narrow corridor I think I can find out if any are armed."

This was done. The entire roomful of people was passed out through a narrow door and this airport police officer stationed himself right in the doorway so that everyone leaving would have to brush by him. In a few minutes he located a prime suspect. When searched, this man was found to be carrying two fully loaded thirty-eight caliber automatics and a live hand grenade. Under questioning he broke down and confessed he intended to threaten the stewardess with a gun and, when she opened the door to the flight deck, he would then display the grenade and threaten to blow up the plane unless they landed in Havana.

As you can see, the executive who received the warning acted in a most intelligent fashion. It would have been easy for him to have transferred at Tampa to a later flight. But fearing impending trouble on the plane, he thought of all the passengers, not only of himself. His subsequent activity saved the entire planeload of people from many hours of fear, anxiety and discomfort, to say nothing of the possibility of complete destruction.

People all over the world are getting warnings like this every day. Some heed them, some do not. If you should get such a warning, give it your attention. Try to see all of its implications. Who knows, you may be able to help others as well as yourself. But do not look for daily guidance, do not seek to depend upon advices and decisions other than your own, for in this you will be surrendering your will to another.

After you have developed a modest degree of clairaudient ability, the next step is telepathy, two-way communication in which you receive and send with equal facility. This will be described at length and techniques for its development will be given in the chapter on telepathy.

PSYCHOMETRY

For as long as man can remember people have known of psychometry and been interested in it. The word itself is not very descriptive. It means "measure of the soul." Actually it refers to making a contact via psychic energy with a person to be studied.

This contact may be with the actual body of the person, such as holding the hand or touching the head, or it may be only a contact with some article which he has carried with him for a length of time.

In attempting a psychometric reading actual physical contact usually is best. Next most efficient is an article of precious metal which has been worn or carried. When a ring, medal, brooch or coin is held in the hand of a sensitive person, the character and present status of the owner can usually be seen and interpreted with accuracy. Often dramatic events of the past will make themselves known and occasionally scenes of the future will disclose themselves. The determining factor in almost every case is the physical condition of the sensitive himself, plus the nature of what is being sought, and the capacity for rapport between the parties. Most palmists and so-called fortune tellers, when they are any good at all, use psychometry whether they realize it or not. The time honored request "First cross my palm with silver," was not only for advance payment and an estimate of the seeker's generosity, but equally that the fortune teller might take in hand a piece of metal which had been carried on the person of the seeker.

A first experience with psychometry

I remember my first experience with psychometry, an experience which surprised me a great deal more than it did anyone else. I was in my early twenties and had been invited to a party where the only person I had ever seen before was the hostess herself. It was during the prohibition era and no alcoholic beverages were served, but the music was good and the food excellent.

While we were waiting for the musicians, who were late, the party dragged a bit and my hostess, in an attempt to stimulate some interesting activity, turned to me and said, "Why don't you read our palms?" I had never done anything like that in my life, but at the time I did not consider it an unreasonable request. So I was seated in an alcove where there was no one behind or beside me and each of the guests came in turn and sat before me.

As I took the hand of the first and looked at the palm I realized I knew absolutely nothing of the art of palmistry. Yet for some reason I felt elated, a sensation I came to know and understand later, and the task I had agreed to seemed quite simple. I looked at the palm of the young man who sat before me and, as I did, a rush of ideas came to me. As rapidly as they came I spoke them aloud and, to my surprise, I soon had a hushed and attentive audience.

Today, I don't recall who the people were, let alone what I said to them, but apparently I was successful in reporting some little known fact to each, and this impressed them. The highlight, which I do recall, came when I told one girl that she was secretly married, which she soon admitted. Since her new husband was also present, the party turned into a wedding celebration and my services as a palmist were no longer required.

The flexible sources for psychometry

The point I make here is that many of us have psychometric ability. Why not explore this possibility? Usually it is necessary to have something on which to focus your attention. This can be the palm of the person you are studying, or it could be a deck of cards from which you could apparently read things, or it could be a coin or some other metal object which had been carried or worn by the subject. Metal is usually better than any other substance. Apparently, the energies which we carry around with us, sometimes referred to as an aura, will cling to garments and articles we wear or carry close to our person. A cotton shirt or a silken blouse will only retain this small bit of energy for a few minutes, but a gold piece or some other article of precious metal will carry impregnated energy for years. Let me tell you an incident which will illustrate this.

> Mrs. R. V. C. is sensitive on several levels and is a very competent psychometrist. Recently at a social gathering, her hostess asked her to do psychometric readings of her guests. Although this was something of an imposition, she graciously agreed. Several people came before her and, because she preferred it, gave her metal articles of various types which she placed on a table before her. She picked these up one by one and held each for a few moments before speaking. Rarely did she examine the article itself. After a succession of rings, pins and bracelets, concerning each of which she

usually said something that brought a surprised response, she picked up an article which, to her, had a strange shape.

Immediately a flood of ideas came to her. She said, "The man who placed this here has not had it very long. There is almost nothing of him attached to it. But it is very old and has a long history. It originally belonged to a man in an eastern country and was used as a mark of his office, a seal. He was an employee of the government, something like a tax collector, and it was required that he stamp with this seal certain articles to indicate the tax on them had been paid. I have no idea how long he lived but from his appearance, dress and mannerisms I would guess it must have been about 2000 years ago."

The man who had presented the article was amazed. It was indeed a seal which he had purchased but a few weeks before in Syria from a workman who had been excavating ancient tombs. This workman had found it encrusted in a ball of mud and had smuggled it away from the diggings to sell on his own.

The point made is that the seal was more deeply impregnated with the aura of the official who had probably worn it on a cord around his neck for years than with any imprint left since then. The workman who found it had it only a few days and certainly never found a use for it. The present owner regarded it as an interesting antique to be kept in a case and only had it with him because he had shown it to the curator of antiquities at the Metropolitan Museum that morning and had been told it was an ancient seal dating back to the first few centuries of the Christian era.

Qualities of psychometry

Most sensitive people are capable of psychometrizing in addition to their other abilities. The Reverend Arthur Ford regards himself as a trance medium, and he is probably the best known and most capable trance medium in the United States, yet he has often psychometrized articles presented to him. Ruth Montgomery, the well known Washington writer, relates in her book *A Search for Truth* how the Rev. Ford once psychometrized a watch she gave him to hold and told her not only that it had belonged to her father but described the symptoms of an ailment he had which was not generally known.

Psychometry is awareness through feeling, knowledge transferred through the sense of touch. It is quite elementary. Almost all of the higher animals possess it to some degree and certainly all humans are capable of it. Because it is so basic, there is no specific training required. It develops in one along with the increase in his psychic energy and only awareness is necessary. I cannot emphasize strongly enough the ever present need to be aware. Do not take things for granted. Do not always accept the obvious, or what seems obvious at the time. We are all far more subtle beings than is generally believed and we respond, often unknowingly, to many urges which are not to be identified under any of the standard labels. For example a Harold W. L. reported the following experience:

I was cleaning out a desk at home when I suddenly thought of a woman, the widow of a friend who had been dead about three years. There was an urge to telephone her and much to my surprise she sounded not only glad to hear from me but asked me if I could stop at her home later that afternoon. When I arrived she wasted no time in coming to the point.

Bringing out a large filing envelope she handed me some papers from it and said "Mike left me a large block of XYZ stock. This has increased in value but the dividends are small. I've been talking to a broker about this and he has suggested I sell it and buy other stocks which would give me a larger return on the money invested. When you called it struck me that I might get your advice and that is why I asked you to stop by. What do you think I should do?"

I looked at the portfolio she handed me and I must confess I was impressed. I had no idea Mike had left such a large estate in stocks. A large portion of the total was represented by 2200 shares of this stock, as she had said. After a little study of her present financial needs I felt she could get sufficient additional income by selling 300 shares of XYZ and putting half of the proceeds, about $50,000, into tax free municipals and the balance into some of the better paying oil stocks, all quite sound. I explained this plan to her and showed how it would mean a net increase of her income after taxes. She was pleased and grateful and said she would follow my advice.

The interesting part of this is that when I returned home

and went back to my desk I found it in the disarray I had left when I had gone to telephone Mike's widow earlier in the day. On the very top of the pile was a case of medals which I had won in various sports over the years. On opening it I found three medals which had been won by Mike many years before and which had in some way become mixed in with mine. Was this coincidence or was it something else?

The subtle power of psychometry

This man has no knowledge of psychometry yet there is in this story strong evidence that the medals belonging to Mike may have triggered the action which he took to benefit Mike's widow. Mike had obviously a high regard for XYZ stock and probably would have disapproved the sale of all of it. So the compromise suggested by Harold offered a most practical solution. But there must have been something other than psychometry at work. What it was and how it worked is not too clear. The resources of our equipment are amazing and worthy of the concentrated study of our greatest scientific minds. Must we wait another hundred years before some scientific group has the courage and enterprise to examine the so-called psychic nature of man? I sincerely hope not.

12

How to Employ Psychic Energy to Send and Receive Telepathic Messages

Telepathic communication is such a frequent occurrence today that even the most materially focussed scientists accept it as factual. This breakthrough into scientific recognition has occurred very recently, actually within the last twenty-five years, and for this reason there is not yet any well-organized index of information on the subject. Most people, when they think of telepathy at all, regard it either as mind reading or as a person-to-person conversation without words, something like a telephone connection on the mental level. Yet these are but two of a great many different manifestations all of which may be classified as telepathic. For simplicity's sake they may be grouped under three general headings as follows:

1. Instinctual telepathy
2. Mental telepathy
3. Soul rapport

HOW INSTINCTUAL TELEPATHY WORKS

Instinctual telepathy is the most common form of telepathic communication. This is not mental at all but involves radiations transmitted and picked up by human beings through the solar plexus. It works most efficiently when actual physical contact exists or when the auras of the subjects are in contact and an interplay of psychic energy occurs between them. However this type of telepathy occasionally does manifest at a distance when impelled by a powerful emotional stimulus.

The first form of communication

Instinctual telepathy was the first and earliest mode of communication which existed between man and man. It antedated speech by many thousands of years. Originally it concerned itself only with self-preservation and reproduction and manifested chiefly as an inner sensation.

Many thousands, possibly hundreds of thousands of years have passed since this was the way we communicated with each other but it is still the widest open door between some undeveloped, non-mental men and women. Their likes and dislikes, needs, desires and aversions are transmitted far more accurately by this ancient, subtle rapport than by the words they have learned to use.

Existing present forms

It also still exists in the attunement between mother and child and it is the manner in which the emotional body of the child is shaped by its parents just as surely as was the physical. This parental and adult influence on children is currently being studied by child psychologists and the conclusion is being forced upon them that the emotional nature of a great many children is imprinted as they grow with the fears, likes and dislikes of their older associates. This sensitiveness of the child to the fluctuating emotional patterns surrounding it may be easily observed. It is not at all unusual for very small children to break out crying when fear or some other emotional shock suddenly strikes the older members of the group, even though they are entirely too young to understand the impending threat.

This same instinctual telepathy is to be observed in the theatre when the "star" sways the audience and makes them laugh or cry. In this case the individuals in the audience exchange emotional reactions with each other in response to the stimulus of the performer. This is one of the reasons why theatre audiences and other similarly emotionally stimulated groups are so apt to panic if fire or any other danger threatens.

This same type of telepathy predominates at a spiritualistic seance. The people are urged to sit close together. Sometimes they are asked to join hands or link arms to form a circle. This facilitates the free flow of psychic energy from one to another throughout the group. Their feelings, worries, sorrows and desires thus become apparent and are introduced as part of the reading.

There is a form of telepathy which operates between some animals and also between certain birds. When migrating birds come to bed down for the night, they do not follow a leader but wheel and land as a unit, just as if they had all simultaneously decided to turn and come down on that particular spot. It is most impressive to observe a large flock of several thousand birds follow this maneuver. Obviously there is a telepathic rapport between them, instinctual telepathy. Dogs and other domestic animals have telepathic communication with each other and are also able to tune in on the simpler emotional reactions of humans.

At one time when my wife and I lived in an apartment in New York City we had a Doberman Pinscher. Although our apartment was on the 16th floor, Jake the Doberman would occasionally rush to a window facing the street and bark furiously almost as if he were defending the home against an enemy invasion. We were completely puzzled by this performance until one day my wife opened the window and looked down to the street sixteen floors below. When she saw a Chow dog being led along on a leash she understood the excitement. Jake had been bitten by a Chow when a puppy and since then had regarded all Chows as enemies. We concluded he was barking at the Chow whom he could not see. Since it was hardly possible that he could smell the Chow through a closed window and at that distance, some other sense must have informed him of its presence.

The case histories of dogs, horses and other animals displaying a response to unspoken wishes and commands of their masters are numerous enough to fill several volumes. This type of communication between man and animal is so common most people take it for granted. It is probably the most obvious form of instinctual telepathy. Even more common, but not so often observed, is the very clear-cut communication between one animal and another. Some friends of mine have two dogs, a standard poodle and a dachshund. The dachshund is younger and a great deal smaller than the poodle but he apparently is the boss. Dog fanciers tell me that this is to be expected since dachshunds are very bossy dogs. For example when this dachshund decides to go to his bed at night he insists that the poodle come along in order to keep him warm. Regardless of what he is doing at the time, the poodle will leave it and quite docilely follow the dachshund to their common bed without a sound or any other noticeable form of communication between them. Thousands of similar examples of instinctual telepathy between animals can be given, but it is better that you seek them out for yourself. In this way the strange and mysterious phenomenon of animal communication will gradually unfold itself before you.

HOW MENTAL TELEPATHY WORKS

Mental telepathy, as the name implies, is communication from mind to mind. This is the telepathic form which concerns us most at the present time and deserves our greatest attention, time and energy. It is my purpose, therefore, to explain it as thoroughly as possible and describe some techniques which, if practiced, will enable you to develop your own telepathic ability. At the very outset I would like to make clear that our objective is to achieve clear-cut accurate communication on the mental level. But because we all have such a large emotional conditioning, it is extremely difficult to free ourselves from it. The more completely emotion and feeling and strong desire are eliminated, the more accurate and successful will be the work accomplished. Even a strong desire to achieve success or a fear of failure will neutralize your best efforts.

Importance of a non-attached attitude

For this reason an attitude of non-attachment or a spirit of "don't care" should be cultivated. This is another way of saying that the attention or the consciousness should be focussed in the mind, or in the brain. It is assumed that the exercises given previously in this book have helped you in this direction. If one were to start from scratch to develop this form of concentration, a great deal of meditative work would be necessary However many people today are already partly prepared for mental telepathy and little extra effort is needed to enable them to function with at least demonstrable skill. Instinctual telepathy is still the easiest path for the greater part of humanity and the intrusion of this possibility must be watched for and guarded against—not that it is wrong or bad but it makes for confusion. The solar plexus is still exceedingly active in most of us and therefore first manifestations are nearly always a mixture of instinctual and mental telepathy. For example the communicator may send a message properly through the throat center (as in oral speech) but the recipient, through habit, will pick it up partly in the mind and partly in the solar plexus.

This can result in an emotional interpretation of the message which was not intended by the sender. Should the sender project the single word "discipline," having in mind only the restraint and training involved in learning mental telepathy, it is possible that the clouded aura of the receiver may supply emotional overtones which are entirely subjective and are not involved in the message itself. Even though he correctly receives the idea of discipline he may surround it with the fear of failure because of a fancied lack of discipline, or the need for greater effort involving almost masochistic overtones (for we are often very cruel to ourselves), or a resentment against circumstances or individuals which he feels may be preventing his achieving the proper discipline. In short he may find himself in a complete emotional turmoil when only the simplest of messages was sent.

Thus you see how important it is to develop your head center by concentration and meditation as a preliminary to the successful practice of mental telepathy. Then it becomes possible to hold the attention in the head and dissolve or drop off all emotional interference. This can be done by the proper application of psychic energy.

Training in mental telepathy can be undertaken by two people who are mutually compatible and who are willing to take turns sending and receiving; or it can be done with a group which should be led by someone already knowledgeable in the art. The group method is probably a little easier because an unconscious attunement between its members activates reception and also because the experienced telepath at its head can direct the course of training in a more skillful manner.

Individual telepathic training

The messages, the thoughts, words, ideas or pictures to be sent should be transmitted both visually and orally on the subjective level. This is because some people will be able to pick up a picture but not a sound while others are exactly opposite. This difference can usually be distinguished in advance by ascertaining the memory type. There are people with visual memories, which is to say they find it difficult to remember anything they have not seen or at least visualized. They will ask you to spell proper names so they can see them written out before their mind's eye much as though they were printed on a blackboard. They can recall how someone looked even though his name is long forgotten. In giving directions they will say "Take the third street to the right and go to the fourth house on the left," and so on. Other people remember sounds better than pictures. When they give directions they are more apt to say "Go to 34 Clark Street" or "Take Main Street." They remember names by likening them to some familiar sound and they can recall verses and songs for years. More advanced telepaths show equal facility with visual and auditory transmissions, but for most beginners it is helpful to start with the technique toward which they are already predisposed. Both methods will be explained.

While there are a great many examples of mental telepathy to be observed today, nearly all of them are spontaneous and not intentional. Our objective is to develop the capacity to transmit and receive messages at will and this requires understanding of the process, plus practical skill in its operation. Certain psychic centers, particularly the head and heart centers, must be consciously employed for consistent results. Likewise both parties must be relaxed and ready. If the receiver is under an emotional strain, he is very apt to be unresponsive, although his intentions are of the best. Or if he should be occupied with a mental problem, he will be encased in a wall of thoughtforms of his own creation, which for the time being will make him impervious to incoming impressions. The same is equally true of the sender.

There are, as you can understand, many problems and pitfalls, so a cultivation of a form of detachment is necessary for success. Because it is not easy to find a trained telepath to act as moderator and with him set up a group, we will first discuss person-to-person telepathy, which requires only two willing collaborators. There is no question but that a good telepathic interrelation can develop without planning between two people who are drawn together by love or mutual respect and admiration. The word love as used here does not mean the physical chemical attraction between the sexes but a spiritual love which recognizes all personality weaknesses and failings but dismisses them as unimportant in contrast with the shining warmth of the inner self. This kind of a relationship is rare, and most of us fall far short of this ideal. But if we wish to learn we must make a start and for this a technique is required.

Steps in successful telepathy

The first step is to realize that we are here dealing with matter and energy just as we do in the physical world. They are just as important in telepathy as they are in operating a telephone system or a broadcasting station. True, we deal with a different type of energy, psychic energy, and a much finer grade of matter, but they are still matter and energy and obey the laws of matter and energy. Always remember this.

In telepathy we deal with

1. the force of love,
2. the force of mind,
3. psychic energy.

1. *The force of love* attracts the needed material with which to clothe the idea, thought, picture or words to be transmitted, thus producing a coherency. You must understand that when you conceive an idea or frame a mental concept, you are actually gather-

ing together and compressing into one place a certain amount of psychic energy on which you have imprinted your idea or message. In order to hold that psychic energy together you must encase it in a capsule or compress it together in some way. This is where the force of love is needed. It causes the elements of the message to cohere to each other for a length of time that is in direct proportion to the amount of love force supplied.

The force of love is also used by the receiver to attract the thoughtform to himself after it has been created and released by the sender. This is done by the would-be recipient focussing his own love upon the sender. You can see from this one fact how difficult a mental transmission would become if even the slightest dislike or disapproval were to exist between the sender and the recipient. It is for this reason I have placed such emphasis upon the need for spiritual love and the avoidance of all criticism.

2. The *force of mind* is used somewhat like a laser beam. Light is a subtle substance and the mind can cause psychic energy to materialize upon a beam of light. This is the most important clue to successful telepathic transmission. A so-called "line of sight" alignment of minds between sender and recipient is necessary. When this has been successfully achieved the message will then travel unerringly to its intended mark. For his part the recipient must exert the magnetic power of love to attract attention, facilitate alignment and create an attunement.

3. *Psychic energy* is the third element required. It reacts and responds to the influence of love and mind and creates an impact upon the vital or etheric body of the recipient from where it is transmitted to his brain and active consciousness.

From the foregoing basic facts we can plan a technique for the sender as follows:

1. He must know the recipient and visualize his or her face and general appearance. After a certain degree of skill and confidence has been developed it is sometimes possible to make a successful connection with a person who has never been seen and whose name alone is known. But at first a good visual imagery is essential.

2. Seek to raise the mind to the mental level and become entirely free of all emotional turbulence.

3. Then visualize the message to be sent. While the word "visualize" is used, it must be remembered that all attempts at transmission must be both visual and auditory. If, for example, you decide to send the word "yellow" you must see the color yellow, see the word "yellow" printed out in large letters and at the same time speak it distinctly. Utter it aloud if you are alone but if not then say it mentally to yourself.

4. As soon as the image is clear in your mind, say the word and send it forth on a wave of love to the intended recipient who has already been visualized.

5. Then dismiss it from your mind and consciousness immediately. This is necessary in order to speed it to its mark. If you continue to dwell upon it you restrain it within your aura, your own mental body, and it cannot break away until you release it by turning your mind from it.

That is the technique, the whole technique. It seems simple, doesn't it? It is simple. The difficult part is in training the mind and emotions to play the right part at the right time. It is no different from learning any other discipline, like playing the piano, or billiards or baseball. The basic ingredients are time, practice and effort.

Helpful hints for development

Here are a few helpful hints. The sender should occupy himself mainly with the clarity of his sending, with the symbol, word or picture, and not with the receiver. A quick glance (so to speak) toward the receiver, a momentary sending forth of love and understanding is usually sufficient to set up a rapport and from there on his attention should be concerned with the visual and audible clarity of the message he is sending.

The receiver should at the outset think briefly of the broadcaster with love or affection, a certain heartfelt warmth, and then dismiss the personality from his mind. The thread of energy linking sender and receiver must be regarded as having been established and considered as existing, then forgotten. It is not too unlike a telephone connection. Once you have dialed the number and heard the answering "hello" you no longer concern yourself with the technique of establishing the connection. You consider it made, ignore it and concentrate on your conversation.

It is also important that the receiver be truly relaxed. Some receivers are so anxious to bring in the message correctly that they tend to block it off by the very intensity of their effort. Try to achieve a "don't care" attitude and remain relaxed and attentive. This is not the strained effort at listening one employs when a suspicious sound is heard in the night. It is more like the casual attention you might give to remarks made by a companion in the next room. The only difference is that instead of focussing on the physical ear you direct your attention to the center of the head where the inner picturing faculty functions. This will facilitate the transmission of the picture or sound from the mind to the physical brain and conscious awareness. It happens occasionally that a successful transmission is made and the brain does not record it at the time of the pick-up but later. This is usually because the receiver's attention is distracted. In such a case the mind retains the impression and releases it into conscious awareness when the attention is not occupied with the more powerful impacts of the physical senses.

The receiver should school himself not to do too much thinking when he expects a telepathic message. It is difficult to restrain the mind and it is this one factor more than any other that will give the new student the most trouble. His mental activity creates its own thoughtforms which can either block out the impulses coming to him from the sender or so scramble them that they lose all intelligibility. He must cultivate a quiescent attitude and a dispassion which desires nothing for his personal self. His thinking process must be slowed down and absolutely nothing of a violent nature be permitted to intrude.

Two compatible people working together regularly, say an hour or two twice a week, can develop a very satisfactory telepathic communion in a few months time. More than this, the sensitivity thus developed will enable them to be aware of the more obvious thoughts of other people with whom they come in contact. Don't misunderstand. It will not permit them to pry into secrets. A person who holds in his mind something he does not wish to be known, puts just as sound a guard about his mind as he does on his lips. But casual thoughts and impressions, ideas that might be spoken, may be readily discerned. Of course, a good telepath will respect the privacy of others and will not attempt to pry into their thoughts. But information intended to be imparted may be picked up instantaneously in contrast to the verbal telling which might take several minutes. Even without telepathic training many people anticipate quite accurately the statements of others. You, yourself, have probably experienced this more than once. You answer a question not yet put into words—to the amazement of the questioner. Or you start to tell something only to have your sentence completed by the person you are talking to. This is perfectly good mental telepathy. Once this endowment of psychic energy is brought under control and employed consciously it will open the doors to a great many other "gifts of the spirit," as St. Paul called them

Group telepathic training

If a trained telepath is available to act as instructor or leader and there are several interested students, a group can be formed. Learning and subsequent development is quicker in group study. When several minds are turned to one thought, a rapport is established and each individual is stimulated thereby. If the group leader is a competent telepath he will know how to conduct each meeting in order to bring the best training to every participant. Nothing can be given here to improve on that "on the spot" direction.

However if a group is ready to assemble and no one has sufficient training to assume the responsibility of instructor, the meeting can still be conducted with profit to each, as follows.

1. Let one of the group be selected or volunteer as leader for one session. Another should assume this responsibility the next time and so on until every member of the group has conducted a meeting. Then repeat.

2. The leader should come to the meeting prepared to transmit visually and audibly. For this he should bring two or three pictures in color and write out three or four one-line slogans or famous sayings such as Patrick Henry's "Give me liberty or give me death."

3. When the group has assembled, the conductor should sit

or stand facing the others and they should all face in his direction.

4. It is assumed that this gathering will be in a room apart and that there will be no intrusions. In order to establish an initial rapport it is usually good to sing a short song which everyone knows or to intone the sound AUM in unison three times. AUM is best sounded on D natural above middle C in a free and natural voice. Be relaxed and easy. This is not a test of singing but merely a technique to establish certain harmonious vibrations which will benefit all.

5. Let the class conductor start with a picture which he plans to transmit visually. Looking at one of the pictures he has provided (it could be a color advertisement from a magazine) he will say to the class, "I will examine this picture and imprint each detail of it in my mind. When I have done this I will then release it when I give the signal. You are then to try to pick it up."

6. After carefully studying the picture, he takes three deep breaths and as he releases the third breath he says, "Now!" At the same time sends the picture out on a wave of love and psychic energy. The visualization must be released so that his mind becomes blank, like an empty motion picture screen.

7. After about a minute he should ask, "Who has picked up anything?" and then urge each one present to tell what he has received. He should encourage each correct observation by saying, "That is correct," or comment on one partially so by confirming the part correctly seen. The errors should be passed over in silence. In the first two or three experiments it is helpful to give a general idea of the picture itself. "It is an outdoor scene" or "It is a picture of a package" or "It is a person" could be offered. Later when the skills are greater these clues should be omitted.

8. After trying two or three pictures, an auditory transmission should be attempted. He should tell the group "This is a well known saying of a hero," or "This is the first line of a well known poem," then read the line to himself. As

he reads he should see each word written on the inside of his forehead. When he comes to the end, he should release it on a wave of love and energy with the outgoing breath and dismiss it completely from his mind.

9. The questioning should follow in a minute and be similar to the probing of the visual sending. It will be found that some students will pick up the verbal transmission more readily than the visual while with others it will be the opposite.

Each sending and its responses should run to about fifteen minutes. Thus possibly two visual and two audible sendings will consume about an hour, which is enough time to devote at first. Do not be discouraged if the initial results are not dramatically successful. They will improve after two or three sessions. This group training is most efficacious and if it is persisted in, success can be pretty much guaranteed for all participants. The rewards are great for one who has trained himself in telepathy. I seriously urge that you endeavor to explore and learn this gift of psychic energy.

HOW SOUL RAPPORT WORKS

Soul rapport is the third general telepathic classification. This exists to a greater or lesser degree between all individuals. As each person achieves a greater refinement and leads a more spiritual life, he gradually becomes more aware of his fellowman. As you train yourself to use psychic energy and employ ever greater surges of this remarkable gift, you will find that your spiritual awareness shows a corresponding improvement. You will become more and more cognizant of all that goes on about you, not only the thoughts and emotions of the people who are close to you, but also the stirring of life in the trees, bushes and flowers, the feelings and intentions of animals, and the great Cosmic calls of wind and rain and tempest. This is the highest human form of telepathy, that of the awakened soul

13

How You Can Achieve Psychic Projection by Employing Psychic Energy

A few years ago, Louise R. had a remarkable experience. She woke up suddenly about 2 A.M. one morning in January and was surprised to see her mother standing at the foot of her bed. As far as she knew her parents were in New York and she was at that time living in West Palm Beach, Florida. Louise noticed that her mother was fully dressed, even to a hat and coat, but she appeared to be standing in an awkward position with both hands out towards her left side.

As soon as she had Louise's attention, her mother said, "Louise, darling, daddy and I are so happy. We have missed you and Charlie so and now we will be together. I can hardly wait."

With this rather cryptic statement, the figure of Louise's mother faded and disappeared. Louise woke her husband who was asleep in the next bed and told him of this strange happening. He did not treat it lightly as she thought he would. She had expected him to laugh at her crazy "dream" and tell her not to eat so much before retiring. But he did not. Instead he questioned her carefully as to how her mother looked and what she was wearing. Then he told her that he had invited her mother and father to spend the winter with them in Florida and indeed expected them to arrive by boat in Miami that very morning. This was to have been a big surprise for Louise and his amazement at her experience was tempered by disappointment that the edge of the surprise had been taken off.

After the sun had come up Louise and her husband drove to Miami and went to the pier where the New York boat was expected. This was before the era of speedy air travel and many people preferred the leisurely and comfortable boat trip to the train ride. They found the boat had arrived and Louise was soon joyfully united with her parents. As soon as the baggage had been collected and all were settled in Louise's automobile, Louise told of her experience the night before.

"Did you see me, mother? Did you do this deliberately? How?" came the rapid questions.

Her mother disclaimed any knowledge of projecting to her daughter, but she explained that she and her husband were so excited at being united with their beloved daughter and her equally loved husband that they could not sleep. They walked the deck of the ship and as they were passing Palm Beach and could identify it by the lights of the hotels, they stood with hands clasped and gazed shoreward.

"Our darlings are there, not more than three or four miles away. I wish we were with them now," her mother had said and recalled that at that moment she fell into a revery thinking of her daughter.

A case of involuntary projection

This is an excellent example of involuntary projection, which is by far the most common type. And it was very successful even though not intended. Her parents were standing on deck and gazing toward the shore. As the ship passed by Palm Beach they were both thinking of Louise and holding each other by the hand. It is interesting that only the mother appeared and her daughter described her just as she was dressed and the awkward way in which she stood. Even though her husband stood at her side and held both her hands he did not become visible or even register on Louise's consciousness. The mother employed more psychic energy, she was concentrating more intently on her daughter and a natural attunement between mother and daughter enabled her to draw upon Louise's psychic energy to create a visible manifestation, a true etheric projection.

Kinds of psychic projection

There are many different kinds of psychic projection. The form just described is most difficult to perform when desired. It is called etheric projection in that the individual uses psychic energy to make himself visible to the person with whom contact is desired. It dresses itself (so to speak) in visible matter at that distant spot while the physical body meanwhile is apparently unchanged and in no way disturbed. There are a great many well authenticated examples of this but nearly all of them were unplanned and came about when the projecting person was asleep, in a revery, or in a trancelike state.

Only seldom does one encounter a successful etheric projection which was planned to be just that. Yet this can be done by anyone with sufficient psychic energy who knows what he wants to do and how to do it. Later in this chapter I will give some suggestions which should enable you to accomplish this if you so desire. But first I wish to tell you about Mental Projection and what you are to do to achieve it.

MENTAL PROJECTION

Mental projection is the easiest and most common form of projection. Most intelligent, thoughtful people frequently send their minds to distant points. They think nothing of this and ignore or discount the impressions they may receive. They do not realize what they have done or know how they did it. But this is a technique which can and should be mastered by everyone who has enough intelligence to solve an algebraic problem or to plan a good dinner. Everyone has the innate ability. It takes but little study and practice to bring it up to a level of awareness where it may be usefully employed at will.

When you start to experiment with mental projection you may think to yourself, "This is just imagination." It is true that, at first, much is imagination—but not all. You must learn by persistent trial and error to distinguish between fantasy and fact. Gradually you will find yourself able to concentrate more and more on the fact and less on the fantasy until ultimately you will be confident that what you observe is a true representation of that which actually has taken place.

How mental projection works

Now let me explain this in a little more detail so you will be sure to understand it. Your mind functions on two levels. For want of better names these are usually referred to as the lower mind and the higher mind. The lower mind functions through the brain while the higher is completely independent of the brain and all other material ties. Normally, we are conscious only in the lower mind. This is where all of the impacts upon our physical senses are recorded, identified, correlated with similar impacts, and then filed for remembrance. All reasoning takes place in the lower mind and we may say that its highest function is to reason carefully, accurately and honestly. The higher mind does not reason. It has access to all information and needs only to observe the fact in order to know it.

But this plethora of evidence, this colossal array of facts, ideas, emotions, and thoughts is most confusing until we learn how to focus in on the information we want. So we usually shut it out entirely and retreat to the lower mind which then resumes its slow plodding from A to B, from B to C, and so on.

This mental slamming of the door is the reason we seldom have any recollection of what was observed during a projection. Now when we start to make a conscious effort to remember, we are going to get interference from our reasoning process. For example, let us say you are in New York and desire to project mentally to your parents in Florida to see if they are well and if they need anything you can supply. You prepare yourself as you have been instructed (and as I will instruct you later) and mentally seek to contact either of your parents. Immediately your reasoning process will start to work. You will think, "It is now

11:30 A.M. It is probably a warm, sunny day and they are no doubt on the beach. I will look for them there."

This is all wrong. You are trying to reason where they are and in doing so you are focussing your attention in your lower mind. This lower mind is indissolubly attached to your physical brain and cannot go anywhere your brain and head do not. In order to project mentally, the higher mind must be used. You must transcend reason. But this is an unaccustomed procedure and some method must be found to detour around the brain and lower mind.

A successful technique

In order to do this, your imagination, a faculty of your higher mind, must be used, but only up to a certain point. When this stage is reached, it too must be winnowed out. Here is one technique which I have found to be successful. There are others.

1. Sit erect in a chair in a room where you are not likely to be disturbed by either intrusion or by extraneous noises.
2. Accumulate psychic energy by taking seven deep breaths. Counting with a regular cadence breathe in to the count of four, hold the breath for the count of twelve, then release it over the count of eight. Do this seven times.
3. While you are holding your breath assemble all of your force as if you were about to lift a very heavy weight. Hold it in tension until you start to breathe out, then relax slowly. Repeat this with each breath. This is one of the best ways for a beginner to accumulate psychic energy.
4. For your first few experiments select a place you know well and have visited in the past. Decide to send your mind there. In order to do this assemble a picture of this place in your mind's eye. For this your imagination must be employed in order that your visualization be as complete and accurate as possible.
5. Hold this visualization for three or four minutes or if not that long, then as long as you can. Try to observe and remember all of the details in the picture. Put yourself in the picture. Get the warmth or cold, the fragrances, the colors. In a word try to feel you are actually there.

6. When you return your attention to the room in which you are sitting, write down all the details you recall. Most of them you inserted yourself through the agencies of memory and imagination. But even on the first try you may be surprised to find certain details which did not consciously originate with you.

Practice this three or four times at a sitting but do not work at it for more than a half hour at the start. In your first few attempts you will notice that you are always partially aware of your physical surroundings, the feel of the chair on which you sit, slight noises from outside, the temperature and the level of light in the room, etc. This is because your attention repeatedly drops back into your lower mind in spite of your best efforts to keep it at a higher level. A rapid vacillation takes place, a flutter in your concentration and, as a result, you are not sharply aware on either level. But if you persist, you will eventually be able to sustain your attention in your higher mind for longer and longer periods. You will succeed in expanding this from fractions of a second, to two or three seconds and then to several minutes. Great mathematicians, champion chess players, composers, poets, and some writers and musicians will often spend fifteen or twenty minutes on this higher level. They do not deliberately seek to focus their consciousness there but their absorption in the work before them leads them out of the physical into the higher mental level. You can learn to do this just as well. But it requires interest, desire and practice.

An alternate successful technique

Now here is a slightly different exercise. It is really the same technique employed in a different way. Let us say you wish to visit an individual and you have no definite knowledge of where he or she may be. Here is what you are to do.

1. Prepare yourself according to steps 1, 2 and 3 in the foregoing exercises.
2. Visualize the face of the person you wish to visit. See only the face and try to see it in clearest detail with all color.
3. As you hold this image in your mind's eye, you will at first

begin to remember the clothes the person wore, how he acted, what he said and did, but pay no attention to these recollections. Let them slide by. Do not arrest them in you thoughts and dwell upon them. They are strictly lower mind or brain memories.

4. Persist in seeing only the face, not the body or actions, and gradually these impressions will begin to fade. As they do, you may pick up a tiny spot of light, or maybe a larger one, somewhere away from the face but definitely in your line of vision. Try to focus in on it. Usually it will seem fairly close to you, almost as if it were suspended in mid-air about ten or twelve inches from your eyes.

5. When you perceive this "intruder" on your otherwise clear picture of the face of the person you are trying to reach, concentrate upon it. You will find that it will appear to expand and include more detail.

6. As this grows, and you should encourage the small spot to expand, you will see that it becomes a definite location like a room, or an automobile, or an open area, and in this location you will see the person you are trying to reach.

7. You will see him as he actually is and in his exact surroundings at that precise moment.

8. Remember, you cannot bring this in by force of will. Once you see the person's face clearly, relax a little. Try to be passive rather than active. You are trying to receive an impression, not create one. So let it come in.

9. One last word on this technique. It will not work if your motive is selfish or unworthy. If you want to spy on someone, you will fail. But if your intention is to learn or to help, you will succeed.

First experience reports

I will include here two reports so that you will get a better idea of how this works and what you may expect. Here is a statement from a Miss T.P. describing her first experience:

I prepared myself as I had been told, then tried to picture my home in Vermont. At first the picture kept changing because I could not make up my mind which view of the house to visualize. Finally I decided on the one from the road and proceeded.

It is not easy to recall a familiar place. You are so used to seeing it that the salient features often elude you. But after a struggle with my memory I finally created a picture which I believe was fairly representative. However one detail baffled me. The weather was clear in Boston and I assumed, naturally, it would be equally sunny in central Vermont. So I visualized my family home with its front porch and large trees bathed in bright sunshine. But the scene shifted. Everything became a dull gray as if a heavy rain was falling. By an effort of will, I brought back the sunny picture but it changed once again to clouds and rain.

At this point I felt baffled and gave up. But when talking to my mother on the telephone the next day she complained about the weather and said, "It's been awful. We haven't seen the sun in three days and most of that time it's been pouring rain."

The foregoing is very good for a first try and Miss T.P. obviously has a previously developed talent which she should work to expand. Now here is a report from a young man who was trying to find his sister who had been missing from their home in Iowa nearly a month:

My sister, Marie-Clair, left home early in December to visit our cousins in Des Moines and do some Christmas shopping. She never got there and we had no word of any kind as to her whereabouts. We contacted the police and gave them pictures and a description and they said they would put out a "missing persons" report on her.

At first we thought she might have been killed but as time went on and we heard of no accidents or tragedies in which she might have been involved, the police said that in their opinion she was alive and had gone off some place of her own free will. She was nineteen years old and well able to take care of herself, they said, but mom and I were not reassured and figured she was dead.

I had been experimenting with mental projection in a half-hearted way but one evening I decided to really try to see if I could find her and determine if she were alive or dead. I did the breathing and got a good picture of her face in my mind, using a photograph to help. It showed her left profile which she always said was her best side.

After ten minutes of trying nothing happened and I was about to give up. As I relaxed I noticed a tiny gleam of light on her left shoulder. When I really turned my attention toward it I could see that it appeared to be hanging in mid-air in front of the visualization and was not part of it. I watched it closely and soon saw it was, or appeared to be, a street light. I let myself drift into the scene as I had been instructed and found myself standing at the edge of water. A street light was before me, the one I had first seen, and away to my right was a marina crowded with all kinds of boats. Standing beneath the street light was Marie-Clair talking to a man. She was dressed in shorts and a T-shirt and was wearing sneakers. But she looked fine and healthy. Delighted, I jumped up and called to my mother, "Marie is alive. I just saw her." She was all excited and asked, "Where? How? Was she on TV?" I explained what I had done and then I was sorry I spoke because mom was so disappointed. She said, "What kind of a stupid fool are you? You have a day dream and get me all worked up over nothing." I was really in bad until three months later when Marie-Clair showed up one evening. She had gone to Florida with a man who had asked her to go with him. "After all, I knew you would never let me go if I asked," she said to mom, "And I knew darned well that if I told you where I was you would want me to come right home. And I didn't want to. Who wants to live in Iowa in the winter? Not me."

Later she confirmed that she had lived on a boat and quite probably had been standing in the exact spot in which I had seen her the night in question. The man she went away with was a small boat captain whom she had met at Thanksgiving time. He had been ordered by the boat's owner to take it from St. Louis down the Mississippi and over across the Gulf to St. Petersburg. Marie-Clair went on the boat with him and lived on board at St. Petersburg until the owner arrived. Then she and Frank, her boy-friend, took an apartment together until it was time to return north.

So I guess I really did see her that time I tried. The boat

was tied up at a marina and there was a large street light where the pier joined the shore. It all seemed to fit correctly.

It is clear that this man was quite successful. A number of circumstances conspired to help. The time was right, neither he nor his sister imposed any mental blocks and apparently he was able to focus his attention sharply enough to get a realization. This is not easy for a beginner.

The mention of mental blocks may need some explanation. If persons desire to keep their actions a secret or if they are occupied with something which normally demands privacy they unconsciously block out a mental approach. Without knowing they do it or intending to, they shut the door to their minds just as positively as they shut the door of a room. But when this man saw his sister she was standing in the open with no more mental barriers than physical around her.

ASTRAL PROJECTION

The projection first described in this chapter, the exercise of Louise, was an etheric projection. This requires a supply of psychic energy at the point where the projection becomes visible to the physical eye. Only a most highly developed and powerful individual is capable of sending that much of his own psychic energy out to a distant point. So most of these etheric projections come about when a person on the spot of the appearance supplies the psychic energy which is there shaped into physical form by the mind of the projector. For this some degree of rapport is required, either voluntarily or involuntarily. Usually an emotional tie, such as existed between Louise and her mother, is all that is necessary.

Soul travel

There has been a great deal written and said recently about soul travel. While actual soul travel may be possible, it is not necessary. When one becomes conscious on the soul level, travel is no longer a factor. What is usually referred to as "soul travel" is really astral projection or travel in the astral body. We all travel in our astral bodies when we sleep but very seldom remember it. It is possible to bring back recollections of these voyages and even to take them at will if we are willing to train ourselves. Here are some suggestions which will enable you to accomplish astral projection. Remember, every human being is different from every other. What one finds easy another cannot do at all. A technique which works for one may not help another and vice versa. So I am giving here several different methods of training. Try them all and pursue the one which you find best.

The physical method. Success is here achieved by establishing a habit pattern of physical action. This is what should be done.

1. Find a place of solitude and relative quiet.
2. Sit erect in a chair with arms and a high back, or lie in bed, preferably the latter.
3. Select a place outside of the room in which you are sitting or lying. Then actually get up and go to that place. It should not be distant. The next room is best. All that is required is to go out of sight of your chair or bed.
4. When you arrive at the selected spot examine it carefully and record in your mind everything you see. You may have been in this room a thousand times before but don't take your knowledge of it for granted. Look about you and carefully catalogue everything in sight and its position relative to everything else in the room.
5. When you have done this return slowly to your chair or bed and at the same time observe everything that is presented to your vision, touch or smell and the order or sequence in which it is presented.
6. Resume your original position in your chair or bed and this time stay there while you go in imagination to the same distant spot and return.
7. When you have completed this imaginary round trip, get up and repeat it in physical action just as you did in numbers 3, 4 and 5.
8. Again repeat this in your imagination and try to observe in your mind's eye everything you saw with your physical sight.
9. For a third time repeat the trip physically and follow it imaginatively. Then discontinue and after an hour's rest

repeat the whole process. If there is not time, then do it again at the next opportunity.

If you continue this method, usually at about the third or fourth sitting as you are returning from an imaginative trip you will be surprised to see yourself sitting or lying apparently asleep in the room whence you started. You will know then that you have accomplished astral projection. Do not be frightened. Go right back to your body, as you did so many times before, and either sit or lie in the position your physical self has assumed. In this way you will automatically join with it once again.

The foregoing physical method is very simple and easy and it will work for a great number of people. However it requires patience, a quality which many lack, and if it isn't your "cup of tea," so to speak, try another.

The *interrupted dream method*. This technique works quite well for certain people while others find it impossible. The only way to know in which category you fall is to try it.

1. The basic assumption is that you dream and can remember your dreams. If you do, then before you go to sleep say to yourself (and really mean it), "When I dream tonight, I will realize I am dreaming."

2. You always dream, everyone does, but sometimes your sleep is so deep you have no recollection of dreaming. Some people say they never dream but actually they do. It is only that on waking they cannot remember. So before you fall asleep instruct yourself to let you become aware that you are dreaming. Usually it is some incongruity in the dream that will alert you. Oliver Fox, in his book *Astral Projection*, states he first became aware he was dreaming when he noticed the tiles in the walk before his home appeared to be laid parallel to the roadway when in actuality they were at right angles to it. When he observed this difference he realized that he was in a dream state.

° Oliver Fox (Hugh Callaway) *Astral Projection*, New Hyde Park. N.Y., University Books, Inc. 1967, pp. 32-33.

Another successful experimenter with astral projection, Beatrice Langley, stated that if she could change the appearance of people in the dream she then knew she was dreaming. But once this was no longer possible and the hair of the red haired woman remained red in spite of all efforts to turn it black, she then knew she had progressed from the dream state to an astral projection.

3. You may take notice of strange abnormalities in a dream and accept them without question, only realizing their incongruity after waking. But if you instruct yourself quite firmly before falling asleep you will soon develop a critical attitude which will enable you to decide while still asleep that this or that appearance is out of character. At this point you will then know you are dreaming.

4. When at some point in your dream you actually "know" it is a dream, you are in a position to take control. Decide then to go to a specific place outside of your room or your home and you will find yourself there in an instant. In describing one of her early experiences, Beatrice Langley said, "I was living in Chicago at the time and before retiring I had given myself instructions in a most positive manner that I was that night to fully realize that I was dreaming. Along towards morning, (it must have been) I dreamed I was walking north on Michigan Avenue. It was late afternoon and a golden sun shone on the Wrigley Building. As I came to the bridge over the Chicago River, I saw that there were beautiful grassy banks on both sides and swans gliding serenely over crystal clear water. At first this seemed quite normal but suddenly I realized what a far cry this idyllic scene was from reality and came to the conclusion I was dreaming. As soon as I realized I was in a dream state my earlier resolution asserted itself and I determined to 'take charge.' I directed myself to go to Paris and instantly I found myself standing in the Place de la Concorde facing the Arc de Triomph. It was early morning of a clear day and the sun was just above the horizon. Everything was amazingly clear and bright and I felt intensely alive and vigorous. I must confess though

that my success surprised and shocked me so that I immediately returned to my body and instantly awoke in bed. It was still dark and a glance at the clock showed it was 2:15 A.M."

5. Your first experience may be exciting and strange, as was Beatrice Langley's. Continue your efforts and before long you will get "the feel" of moving about in the astral body. Then you should be able to release yourself from the physical without the need to first sleep and dream.

The next method I describe requires the use of the will and what is termed a *"one-pointed control."* When the practice of either of the two techniques here given (or of any other technique known to you) has made you adept, you can then release your astral body at will, given the proper conditions. There are many people alive today who have learned in previous lives to travel in the astral world. You may be one and have this gift lying dormant within you waiting to be reawakened. The only way to determine this is to try. Here is the method:

1. Select a place where you will not be disturbed. This is important. You are about to induce a trance-like state in your physical body and any sudden shock can be damaging to your heart and nervous system. A loud voice, a slamming door, a touch upon your body will cause a rapid return of your astral body to the physical which is almost as if it had dropped into it from a height of ten feet. So be careful.

2. Lie upon a bed or couch. Keep on your clothing but loosen anything that is tight or presses upon you. Do not get into bed. This is associated with sleep and you do not want to sleep. You are about to enter a trance-like state which is akin to sleep but in which you maintain a continuous conscious awareness.

3. Close your eyes and relax but be sure to stay awake. When relaxed take five deep breaths in order to increase your quota of psychic energy. Breathe as follows, counting to yourself in a regular cadence. Breathe in deeply to the

count of four. Hold your breath for the count of twelve, then breathe out to the count of eight, all in the same cadence. Do this five times.

4. When you have finished the breathing exercise you will feel stimulated and alert. Turn your consciousness then to the pineal gland. This is in the center of your head back of the root of the nose and about on a line with the upper part of your ears. Feel it glow with the psychic energy your attention focuses upon it.

5. Shut out all sights, sounds and other physical impacts as you concentrate all of your attention on this tiny gland. Feel it glow with fiery energy and as you do lift it in consciousness up to the ceiling.

6. When you feel you have succeeded in lifting the pineal gland up and out of the body, permit yourself to become aware of your surroundings once again. In most cases you will find yourself hovering four or five feet over your body, which appears to be sleeping. In some cases you will be already out of the house and high in the air. Do not panic. Do not become unduly excited but quite calmly direct yourself by an action of the will to go wherever you desire. It is merely like saying "I would like to go to my office" or "I would like to go downtown" or "I would like to go to my mother's." Instantly you will be there.

7. Some experimenters have found pleasure in moving their astral body slowly once they found themselves free of the physical. There is a definite exhilaration in moving about in the astral world. You feel very free and light and can glide along quite slowly or rush over land and sea at speeds which seem to approach the speed of light. It is up to you to decide.

8. While it is your will that directs your astral body's motion, sometimes it is difficult for the student to accept this. Then it is practical to start with some recognized method of physical locomotion. You can swim or walk or run. But soon you will find that these illusions are not necessary and give them up.

1 remember in one of my earliest experiences I was fortunate to be one of a group who were being instructed on the astral plane by a guide or teacher. As part of our training, he took us on a flight over water. On looking down at the storm tossed ocean so close below me, I panicked. The guide was keenly aware of my emotional reaction and with a swift movement that seemed like sleight-of-hand, he produced a long surf-board and, as he placed it beneath my body, said smilingly, "Lie on this, then, if you must." This caused no little amusement among the others who already knew how useless such a prop actually is except as an emotional reassurance.

The three techniques here given will enable most of you to achieve astral travel if you approach them seriously and with persistence. There are many other ways, some of which will reveal themselves to you as you experiment. Others you can learn from reading and study. Before leaving the subject, a word should be said about the astral plane, the world in which astral travel takes place.

CHARACTERISTICS OF THE ASTRAL PLANE

The astral plane is vast and covers many vibratory levels. At its lowest level it almost parallels the physical and it is here that most of our astral travel takes place. At its highest level the astral plane is very rarefied and few ever reach there while still in physical incarnation. Of course there are an infinite number of levels in between.

The human astral body is not the only traveler on the astral plane. You will find many other forms there, some attractive and some menacing. Do not permit any to frighten you or disturb your peace of mind. Remember, you have the power of control of astral entities just as surely as you have the power to control your emotions. But if you are not able to control your emotions you will be unwise to attempt an astral voyage until you have achieved this competence. Then do not content yourself with earth level trips, entertaining though they may be, but lift yourself up to the higher levels. There you will be stimulated mentally and physically and return refreshed in every way. These benefits alone are worth your every effort.

14

How to Employ Psychic Energy to Raise Your Consciousness to Higher Levels

In earlier chapters I have used the simile of a house with three or more levels to illustrate the different planes of consciousness on which we may function. Most people are happily content to live, think and act on the lowest level and never have a moment's desire to lift themselves up from it. But a person like yourself, interested in gaining understanding and the power it gives, will want to raise his consciousness as high as possible. So in this closing chapter I will show you how to do this.

Every religion tells you to "lift your thoughts to God." Every esoteric school says "raise your consciousness." These injunctions are sound. They advise the performance of a physical act, lifting, which if attempted with energy and a good accompanying visualization will result in a raising of the vibratory level of your being. A thought raised upward is visible in the astral light as a spire thrusting aloft, with wisps of etheric and emotional energy trailing down from its tip. The maypoles of old, festooned in many colored streamers, were not the phallic symbols many consider them to be but attempts to represent the uplifted thoughts of men as seen from the psychic side—for each thought lifted out of the mundane will carry with it, and seemingly dripping from it, some of the emotional substance of its creator.

The great cathedrals of the world, with their tall steeples reaching in upward cascades toward the sky, are evidence of the intent of their designers to reproduce in stone what they have observed in the astral-etheric substance. Five or six hundred people in a group gathered for religious service will send up a mighty pylon a quarter of a mile into the sky. From its peak it will broaden downward in increasingly fuller cascades to the aura of the group which created it. Over every dedicated group, whether it be but three or three thousand, may be seen this same astral manifestation, large or small, depending upon the number present and the intensity of their aspirations.

It is a recognition of this psychic manifestation which has led to the injunction "Lift up your thoughts." The very effort to lift your awareness out of the body to some point in the air above results in a raising and in a speeding up of your vibratory rate. But like the water in the fountain, it falls back again at once unless a technique is used to sustain it at a higher level. It is important that you learn how to do this and that as many people as possible learn it. So I will do my best to teach you.

BENEFITS OF RAISING YOUR CONSCIOUSNESS

A sincere raising of the consciousness gives us a view, a look at the Cosmic scheme, a realization of what may lie before and beyond us, but when we return to the physical level we are men and women once again with human appetites and tendencies and all the problems they create. We must eat, sleep and die. It is for this reason we must also strive to raise the vibratory level of our physical-atomic substance. Then each time our consciousness returns from a flight into the Infinite it will occupy a better, a finer vehicle. This is the true road to development.

There is an amazing plan for humanity created by God, or the Cosmic, or the First Cause, whichever designation you prefer,

that is at this time swinging into action. In order to fully appre-
ciate it you must be willing to set aside many long-held ideas about
the way a human being is constructed and the way his equipment
works—or at least withhold your judgment until you give a good
honest try to some of the training methods in the earlier chapters.

I urge you therefore to practice telepathy or astral projection
or even dowsing. By all means learn one of these techniques.
Success with any one will open your eyes and enable you to understand in some measure this magnificent plan.

ENERGIZING FACTORS INVOLVED

Nothing as colossal as this can be done overnight and specific
preparations were started many hundreds of years ago. All of the
rapidly changing and disturbing conditions in the world at this
time reflect the working out of these preparatory influences. The
energizing factors involved may be described as follows:

1. The turbulence caused by the passing of the influence of
the Piscean Age with its emphasis on authority and unquestioning
belief, and the coming into manifestation of the energies of the
Aquarian Age which demand direct knowledge and encourage
"do-it-yourself" tendencies.

2. The 63-year worldwide conflict which started actually in
1912 and will not finally end until 1975. This marks a climax in
the history of mankind and the subjective effect it has upon the
nervous systems of men and their astral bodies has not yet been
fully grasped. The increase in the sound level (contributed to in
many ways) and the intense emotional strain of the prolonged
conflict has torn the web of etheric matter which separates the
physical and astral worlds. Now the surprising process of uniting
these two worlds is beginning. Vast changes in the human consciousness are taking place. Eventually this will lead to human
understanding and a realization of the true brotherhood of men,
but the path is not an easy one. The stimulation involved is impersonal and a great many will use these energies for evil rather
than good. Control and discipline are essential. I warn you, do
not let loose a whirlwind you cannot stop.

3. Certain astrological relationships between the constellations are releasing new types of force, hitherto unknown to this earth. These forces are making possible many developments in the human psyche and personality which, up until now, have been inhibited and frustrated. Latent powers and new knowledge will be rediscovered and employed. You have the capacity to use some of this force to your own advantage and to the benefit of the world, if you will.

THE IMPORTANCE OF DEVELOPING YOURSELF WITH PSYCHIC ENERGY

In days to come certain highly trained and dedicated men and women will make their appearance in various parts of the world. Their purpose is to help humanity. They will teach, they will demonstrate, they will advise and give example. Their very presence will have a beneficent effect. But do not wait to be summoned by one of these Masters of Wisdom. Start now to develop yourself.

THE OBJECTIVES OF THE MASTER PLAN

You may ask, and rightly so, "What is the objective of this plan? You have described the conditioning process. What will be the result if it is successful?"

The object is 1) to produce such an attunement between men that a perfect telepathic interplay will result. As you can realize, this will eventually annihilate time or at least our understanding of it; and 2) to so raise the human vibratory level that most men will be able to progress to the third level of understanding where there is available to their scrutiny and study all past achievements and knowledge. Man will then know the true significance of and the possibilities inherent in his mind and brain and thus open the door to a God-like omniscience.

These objectives are not to be realized in the dim and distant future. There are some men and women who are already beginning to open these long-closed doors. You can join this group— IF YOU WILL. The price of membership is not high. No money is required. The only payment is a willingness to study and work with persistence, a willingness to always put the welfare of your brother before your own and the ability to pick yourself up and start again, and again, and again.

HOW TO GET FULFILLMENT OF YOUR DESIRES

Now, join with me in one last exercise, an exercise I hope you will perform every day for the rest of your life. It will do everything for you that you want and need. I need say no more. Now sit back and relax as we begin.

1. Center your consciousness in your heart and visualize your entire chest area enveloped in a pink aura.
2. Take in a breath to the count of six while you hold this visualization.
3. Hold your breath in for a count of twelve and as you do so raise the pink cloud to a point about three inches above the top of your head.
4. Release your breath slowly to the count of eight and at the same time expand the pink cloud so that it includes your head and the upper part of your body.
5. When your breath is expelled and your lungs are empty, hold your breath out to the count of twelve and at the same time keep in your mind's eye the visualization of the shining pink cloud surrounding your head and upper body.
6. Now, center your consciousness in your throat and visualize a bright blue aura enveloping your throat and shoulders.
7. Take a breath to the count of six and hold the visualization of the blue aura.
8. Hold your breath in for a count of twelve and as you do raise the blue aura to a point about three inches above the top of your head.
9. Release your breath slowly to a count of eight and at the same time expand the blue cloud so that it includes your head and the upper part of your body.
10. When your breath is expelled and your lungs are empty

hold your breath out for the count of twelve and at the same time maintain the visualization of the bright blue aura enveloping your head and upper body.

11. Now, center your consciousness in your pituitary gland. This is in the skull right above the bridge of the nose and between the eyebrows about one-half inch back of the forehead. As you do, visualize a brilliant white light around your head and count six while you breathe in.

12. Hold your breath for a count of twelve and raise the white aura to a point about three inches above the top of your head.

13. Release your breath to the count of eight and as you do so feel the pituitary center join with the center above your head so that they become as one while the light created by this fusion lights up the whole room.

14. When your breath is expelled hold your lungs empty for the count of twelve and see that brilliant sun-like aura expand so that it includes your head and the entire upper part of your body above the waist.

15. Relax and sit in quiet meditation for about three minutes. During this period petition for what you need. If it is a worthy petition it will be granted. Before you rise say to yourself "Let good befall the world."

CONCLUDING REMARKS

In this book I have given you some exercises and techniques to work with and I hope I have encouraged you to explore their possibilities. I also hope you will come to realize that your own development, desirable though it may be, is not enough. Psychic energy should be studied in schools and the pupils taught how to apply it. Scientists should devote as much time, energy and money to understanding psychic energy as is currently being poured into the exploration of space. When this energy is better understood, space exploration will become simple. The future is vast and wonderful beyond our most vivid imaginings. For those who plant its seeds, the rewards are great.